Sri Krishna Yoga

Lectures by

SWAMI SARVAGATANANDA

Compiled and Edited by

BIJOY MISRA

Advaita Ashrama
(Publication Department)
5 Dehi Entally Road
Kolkata 700 014

Published by
Swami Mumukshananda
President, Advaita Ashrama
Mayavati, Champawat, Uttaranchal
through its Publication Department, Kolkata
Web-site: *www.advaitaashrama.org*
E-mail: *mail@advaitaashrama.org*

First Edition, October 2005
3M3C

Cover Design/Graphics:
Nilay Deshmukh

Cover picture:
Parthasarathi Krishna by Nandalal Bose

ISBN 81-7505-276-7

Printed in India at
GRAPHOEB
Kolkata 700 059

This book is dedicated to the memory of Swami Ranganathananda, the late President of the Ramakrishna Math and Ramakrishna Mission, who was instrumental in bringing the book to publication.

The shrine in the chapel at
Massachusetts Institute of Technology in Cambridge, MA.
The 'Sri Krishna Yoga' lectures were delivered here during the
Independent Activities Period in January 1997.

'It shares with the great faiths opportunities for furthering man's spiritual understanding' — *James R. Killian, President, MIT, 1954.*

Contents

Publisher's Note

The present book, *Sri Krishna Yoga,* is a collection of essays taken from lectures on the subject of Yoga as taught by Sri Krishna in the *Bhagavad Gita.* The lectures were delivered at the Massachusetts Institute of Technology and several other places in the USA by one of the seniormost and venerable monks of the Ramakrishna Order — Swami Sarvagatananda, formerly Spiritual Minister of the Ramakrishna Vedanta Society, Boston, and the Vedanta Society, Providence. When these lectures were originally delivered they were followed by lively question-and-answer sessions, and the questions and answers have been retained in this work at the end of each chapter.

The word Yoga means 'to join — that is, to join us to our reality, God. There are various Yogas, or methods of union, but the main ones are Karma Yoga, Bhakti Yoga, Raja Yoga and Jnana Yoga' (*Complete Works of Swami Vivekananda,* Vol. 5, p. 292).

Regarding the central theme of the *Gita,* Swami Vivekananda once said: 'Though before its advent, Yoga, Jnana, Bhakti, etc. had each its strong adherents, they all quarrelled among themselves each claiming superiority for his own chosen path... It was the author of the *Gita* who for the first time tried to harmonize these. He took the best from what all the sects then existing had to offer and threaded them in the *Gita*.... The reconciliation of the different paths of Dharma and work without desire or attachment — these are two special characteristics of the *Gita*' (Ibid., Vol. 4, pp. 106-7).

In this volume revered Swami Sarvagatananda has explained the teachings of the *Gita* in his masterly and illuminating way. While following the outline of Swami Vivekananda's thoughts, he has presented a new approach with some original ideas — particularly in the chapter 'Sri Krishna Yoga'. These ideas have then been elaborated in subsequent chapters. We believe readers all over the world, irrespective of caste or creed, will find this exposition of the *Gita* intellectually stimulating and spiritually invigorating.

Kolkata PUBLISHER
16 July 2005

Foreword

Did Sri Krishna teach a doctrine in the *Bhagavad Gita*? Swami Sarvagatananda discovers and analyses Sri Krishna's powerful message of harmonious living and spiritual awakening. *Sri Krishna Yoga* is a synthesis of paths that complement each other with a goal towards human perfection.

'This book *Sri Krishna Yoga* was read to me by a monastic brother. I suggest that the book be published and then sent to all the American centres, as also to London, Singapore, Sydney, and Tokyo centres…

'I say, "Go onward."'

Swami Ranganathananda
13th President
Ramakrishna Math & Ramakrishna Mission

Pronunciation Guide for the Transliterated Sanskrit

The book contains quotations from the *Gita* in Roman transliteration. This table gives hints for pronouncing the transliterated Sanskrit words. All Sanskrit characters are phonetic and the transliterated alphabets would sound like:

a like *o* in *come*
ā like *a* in *far*
i like *i* in *bit*
ī like *ee* in *feel*
u like *u* in *full*
ū like *oo* in *cool*
ṛ like *ri* in *ring*
e like *a* in *cake*
ai like *i* in *mite*
o like *o* in *note*
au like *ou* in *count*
ṁ like *m* in *some*
ḥ like *h* in *half*
k like *k* in *kite*
kh like *kh* in *silk-hat*
g like *g* in *go*
gh like *gh* in *long-hut*
ṅ like *ng* in *sing*
c like *ch* in *church*
ch like *chh* in *church-hill*
j like *j* in *jug*
jh like *dgeh* in *hedgehog*
ñ like *n* in *singe*
ṭ like *t* in *curt*
ṭh like *th* in *hot-house*
ḍ like *d* in *bird*
ḍh like *dh* in *red-hot*
ṇ like *n* in *bond*
t like *t* in *three*
th like *th* in *thunder*
d like *th* in *though*
dh like *the-h* in *breathe-hard*
n like *n* in *pen*
p like *p* in *pun*
ph like *ph* in *top-hat*
b like *b* in *bat*
bh like *bh* in *abhor*
m like *m* in *man*
y like *y* in *young*
r like *r* in *rust*
l like *l* in *lump*
v like *v* in *levy*
ś like *sh* in *ship*
ṣ like *sh* in *should*
s like *s* in *sun*
h like *h* in *home*
' stands for an *elided a*

Introduction

Yoga is the means and the end, the way and the goal. The sage Patanjali defines it as *cittavṛttinirodhaḥ*, 'It is the control of all the tendencies that arise from the subconscious mind' (*Yoga Sutras*, I. 2). A human being is a beautiful blending of three elements (the animal, the human and the divine) and is endowed with many faculties. In all the three dimensions, the individual is struggling to grow and evolve. The right way to evolve is yoga. Yoga teaches us how to control all sides of ourselves: the physical, the mental, the moral, the intellectual, and the spiritual. All these realms must be properly balanced and controlled. Any spiritual discipline that helps us to evolve and gain an element of spiritual perception has been called a yoga.

Next, we have to consider yoga as the goal and as the end. Patanjali has mentioned that yoga is unity with the ultimate ground. In the last chapter, he describes the sixth dimension of samadhi, called *nirbījasamādhi*, 'seedless samadhi'. Samadhi comes from Sanskrit words *sama* and *adhi*. *Adhi* means 'the highest', *sama* means 'equal'. Samadhi means equating ourselves with the highest. When the individual consciousness, having evolved slowly, enters into the cosmic realm and becomes one with it, the individual is totally lost in the cosmic. Sri Ramakrishna used to give a beautiful example: 'The salt doll wanted to measure the depth of the sea. It entered into the sea and melted away. There was no trace of it. The doll became one with the sea.' Such is the case with our individual consciousness. When it is purified, it becomes one with the cosmic conscious realm. Yoga as the end has the ultimate goal of achieving oneness with the Divine Ground.

All saints and sages, both in the East and in the West, ancient and modern, are yogis. Two elements exist in all of them. The first is controlling the mundane sense perceptions and evolving to the higher realm. The second is turning the mind to something spiritual. Let us take the case of Moses. What did Moses do? He moved to the mountain and entered his spiritual search. He moved from the sensual realm to the transcendental realm. He moved up. He saw a vision, and heard a voice. The same conditions were repeated with Mohammed. He moved away from society, fasted and prayed. He received the awareness of the Cosmic Being whom he called Allah. He also heard a voice. Similarly, Jesus Christ retreated to the wilderness. He struggled hard, contemplated and prayed. He received a similar awareness. Not only did he hear the voice, he received a revelation. He said, 'I and my Father are One' (John, 10:30). That unity of the individual and the cosmic is the end of yoga. Zarathustra, Buddha, Confucius, Lao Tzu — all these great souls are yogis. They controlled and conquered their minds. They received revelations.

Everywhere now, the word 'stress' is commonly used. Stress is due to many factors: pressure from work and pressure from various life situations — failing to cope with society. All these pile up. The individual loses his ground. Doctors and therapists are recommending yoga and meditation as a remedy. Slowly yoga is entering everyday life.

Three thousand years ago, on the eleventh day of the bright fortnight in the month of *Mārgaśīrṣa* (November-December), Sri Krishna started giving instructions to Arjuna. Those instructions fortunately have been well recorded and have come down to us in the form of the *Gita*. The *Gita* presents to us a beautiful concept of yoga. Sri Krishna is *yogeśvara* — the master of yoga. The *Gita* is called *yogaśāstra*. Sri Krishna is the best example in practice from the point of view of the teachings of yoga. He is well balanced, well integrated and completely identified with the highest.

The *Gita* is spiritual dynamics. The whole *Gita* is nothing but yoga and a discourse on yoga. Sri Krishna calls yoga a discipline, a process that can help us gain depth. Then he gives us his own doctrine which is a synthesis of all the processes. As for the means to the end, or the way to the goal, we need guidance. In all the chapters of the *Gita*, we find this guidance, and Sri Krishna is the guide.

May He who is Heaven of the Christians, Holy One of the Jewish Faith, Allah of the Muslims, Buddha of the Buddhists, Tao of the Chinese, Ahura Mazda of the Zoroastrians, Great Spirit of the Native Americans and Brahman of the Hindus lead us from the unreal to the Real, from darkness to Light, from death to Immortality. May the All Loving Being manifest Himself unto us and grant us abiding understanding and all consuming divine love. Peace, peace, peace be unto all…

— Sunday Prayer at Ramakrishna Vedanta Society of Boston

Sri Krishna Yoga

The scene of the *Gita* is a battlefield. Assembled are hundreds of soldiers and generals on either side. All are kinsmen skilled and equipped to vanquish the opposing side with strength and valour. One side is called the Pāṇḍavas. It consists of the five sons of the deceased Pāṇḍu and their allies. The other side is called the Kauravas. It consists of the one hundred sons of the blind Dhṛtarāṣṭra and their allies. Pāṇḍu and Dhṛtarāṣṭra were brothers and the battle is fought by the cousins to gain control over their ancestral land. Duryodhana, the eldest of the Kaurava brothers, is determined to keep the Pāṇḍavas out of the land. The Pāṇḍavas have negotiated and failed. Duryodhana would not compromise. He has set his mind to win or perish. The softhearted Arjuna, who is the middle brother among the Pāṇḍavas, enters the battlefield driven by his teacher and charioteer Sri Krishna. The unseemly sight of kinsmen ready to kill each other perplexes Arjuna. He expresses his emotions and sorrow. He asks clarification on his duties and values. Sri Krishna explains. This is how the *Gita* is set up as a philosophical text. Arjuna puts the following question to Sri Krishna:

Kārpaṇyadoṣo'pahatasvabhāvaḥ
pṛcchāmi tvām dharmasammūḍhacetāḥ;
Yacchreyaḥ syānniścitam brūhi tanme
śiṣyaste'ham śādhi mām tvām prapannam — 2. 7

'I am lost. I am bewildered and confused. I do not know where I am or what to do. I am your disciple and you are my guide. Please tell me for certain what should I do.' The question is concerned with the issue of duty, conscience and obligation. Sri Krishna consoles Arjuna with the knowledge of the soul, the body and that of life and death. He presents the philosophical discourse of Sānkhya. He enunciates the eternity of the soul and the transient nature of the body. He presents the idea that death is a transformation, and that our actions in the world are determined by our ability to discriminate righteousness from unrighteousness. We are dutiful soldiers in the battle of life. We have little control over success and failure of our efforts. Hence the message: we should do our tasks and accept victory or defeat in complete equanimity.

ENUNCIATION OF SRI KRISHNA YOGA

The enunciation of the message is beautifully composed in the thirtieth stanza of the third chapter of the *Gita* and is the essence of the teaching. Sri Krishna says:

Mayi sarvāṇi karmāṇi
saṁnyasyādhyātmacetasā;
Nirāśīrnirmamo bhūtvā
yudhyasva vigatajvaraḥ — 3. 30

'Surrendering everything to me and removing all mental fever, greed and egotism, fight using your spiritual consciousness.' There are several keywords in the statement. Each attribute is important. Analysis of these attributes is necessary and important.

Together they make the perfection of human qualities that can be considered as the doctrine of Sri Krishna. As he would say later, the doctrine is old and has been passed down through generations by the wise.

SURRENDERING EVERYTHING TO 'ME'

Mayi sarvāṇi karmāṇi saṁnyasya, 'Surrendering everything to Me' is the most important phrase in the stanza. Who is 'Me'? 'Me' is the Inner Will, the God within. Sri Krishna proclaims himself as the Divinity and propounds the invocation of surrender. Through this declaration, Sri Krishna transforms himself as the ultimate refuge and establishes his identity with the Divine Cosmic Being, the cause of all events. Sri Krishna metaphorically becomes the Inner Will that resides as God in every heart. It is our ultimate support. 'Surrender everything to Me' should be transposed as 'surrender everything to God'.

The keyword is surrender. Actions do not belong to us. We are mere instruments of design available to implement the actions. There are no individual actions, but there is only collective fulfillment of our individual duties. These duties are best performed when surrendered to God. Our duties are prescribed to us by circumstances through a larger design that we do not comprehend. Our actions may or may not have the results that we might like. However, we can concentrate on performing the actions with diligence and make all our efforts an offering to God. He advises us to surrender *everything* to God.

With Spiritual Consciousness

Sri Krishna says that our surrender should be *adhyātmacetasā*, 'with spiritual consciousness'. What is in 'me' pervades all equally. No 'object' is unique. In all of us there is the same Self, the same soul, the same Spirit of Allah, the same Kingdom of Heaven. All we have to do is to recognize it. We have to develop our consciousness. With spiritual consciousness, all shapes blend and merge, all faiths become a path of the Inner Will, every object becomes divine. When we surrender everything to God, we do so with spiritual consciousness. Such consciousness transcends our personal faith perceptions.

Adhyātmacetasā literally translates to 'with the complete knowledge of one's own Self'. Our actions are spiritual. By engaging in actions with complete spiritual consciousness we are able to offer them to God. When we discover the nature of the Self, we don't distinguish between objects, and we observe the inclusion of everything in our Self, thus making us spiritually sensitive to all sensory objects.

Without Greed

Then we have *nirāśī*, 'without any greed'. We have to learn what greed does, and where it takes us. Greed is a great evil in life, particularly in our families and in our social interactions. Our actions must not be the fulfillment of our greed, but rather duties that are surrendered to God. We must not be selfish in our actions; we must be dutiful. We must accomplish our actions with spiritual consciousness. Then nothing we do may breed greed in us.

Doing any work with selfish motive is greed. Greedless action forbids us from indulging in activities of which we are the beneficiaries. Our actions must demand a collective gain, not an individual gain. In the spiritually conscious world, the individual's benefits are tied totally to the universal benefit. The individual exists only with the whole. The individual has a personal duty that must be conducted with spiritual consciousness.

WITHOUT EGOTISM

The next word is *nirmama*, 'without any egotism'. No action is our own. Hence there is no ownership of any action. When all actions are surrendered to God, we do not own any of the results. This requires that all actions must be performed without any ego. Egolessness makes the actions objective and without bias. Our services become universal. They are not confined to any limited boundaries. The universality of action makes us respectful to all creatures, and creates in us a loving relationship with everything. Our vision transcends limited social horizons and we see the divinity in our nature and work. Egoless actions performed without greed and with complete spiritual consciousness are surrendered to God.

Egolessness is an attribute in our actions when we do not own the latter. This happens when we consider ourselves as 'agents' of tasks rather than the 'doers' of the tasks. We engage in the execution of a task because the task needs execution, but we do not assign the task to ourselves, neither are we concerned about the ultimate outcome. We accomplish our share of duties with love and respect. We do not harbour ill feelings against any one though we fight against misconduct. We protect ourselves from selfish misdeeds so that we can uphold nobility and the virtue of righteousness. We use our faculties of discrimination to act on behalf of God and all our actions are offerings to God.

WITHOUT MENTAL FEVER

The next attribute is *vigatajvaraḥ*, 'without any mental fever'. Life contains excitations and anxieties, which create the feverish condition of the mind. Except for the period when we are in deep sleep, various disturbances play through the mind. These disturb the peace of mind, letting it accumulate 'fever'. We must relieve the mind of its fever while we are engaged in action. Indeed, anxieties can be eliminated with spiritual consciousness and we are at peace when they are removed. Surrendering our actions to God requires that we remove our anxieties and be relieved of any mental fever.

Anxieties in the mind are caused by our association with the consequences of our actions, thereby disturbing our peace of mind. In order to be at peace with ourselves we must rid ourselves of these mental excitations. All conflicts in our mind must be resolved and removed before we can concentrate on the steps required for the execution of our tasks. A spiritually conscious person has no mental anxiety. As we proceed to make ourselves spiritually conscious, mental anxiety must diminish. The spiritual offering of our actions requires that they be performed with a pure mind and with a completely peaceful sense of discrimination.

FIGHT!

Sri Krishna teaches that we should equip ourselves with the prescribed attributes and participate in life's battle. He declares that one must engage in this battle with spiritual consciousness and he commands — *yudhyasva*, 'fight!' In these battles, there are no winners or losers; we have the duty of participation only. Any personal gain is illusory. God decides the steps. A yogi acts and surrenders all actions to God.

All actions in life are battles of different kinds. Sri Krishna proposes that all battles must be fought with full spiritual consciousness. The battle of life is one of action and all actions must be performed without greed, egotism and mental anxiety.

THE FOUR YOGAS OF THE GITA

The practice of the above doctrine of Sri Krishna demands the perfection of our faculties. All the faculties — thinking, feeling, willing and restraining — must be perfected. Perfecting thinking is achieved through Jnana Yoga, perfecting feeling is achieved through Bhakti Yoga, perfecting willing is achieved through Karma Yoga, and perfecting restraining is achieved through Raja Yoga. *Mayi sarvāṇi karmāṇi saṁnyasya*, 'dedicate all works to me' is Bhakti Yoga; *adhyātmacetasā*, 'with spiritual consciousness' is Jnana Yoga; *nirāsīrnirmamo bhūtvā yudhyasva*, 'fight without greed, and egotism' is Karma Yoga; and *vigatajvaraḥ*, 'without any mental fever' is Raja Yoga. The combination of these four yogas leads to human perfection. Striving towards such perfection is the goal of the *Gita*. Sri Krishna's message is that we must aim to create a way of life where such perfection is achieved.

'Surrender everything to God' does not point to God in any particular faith. You resign everything to God as you feel from within. You surrender to the higher power according to your own belief, conviction, and practice. We have come to this world as transient travellers. We know very little about the world. What we can infer is that there is a design behind our actions. We can call it by any name. God has many names: 'as many religions, so many names'. Our surrender is to the name. That name exists in all of us.

Sri Krishna continues:

Ye me matamidaṁ nityam
anutiṣṭhanti mānavāḥ;
Śraddhāvanto'nasūyanto
mucyante te'pi karmabhiḥ — 3. 31

'Men who constantly practice this doctrine of mine with faith and without vanity, they too are liberated by doing actions.' Here he declares *me mataṁ idaṁ*, 'this doctrine of mine', thus personalizing the doctrine as his own.

LIBERATION FROM THE BONDAGE OF WORK

Worldly actions are always followed by newer actions, and so we have the bondage of actions. When we surrender our actions, we are liberated from the bondage. While our actions must be unselfish and devoid of expectations, our surrender should be with faith and without vanity. We need to practice faith every day.

The above is the only verse where the identification of the doctrine with Sri Krishna is spelled out. The doctrine is a call for action for the individual. It enunciates non-greed and unselfishness as fundamental values in spiritual practice. The doctrine is a path to perfection that enjoins the cultivated exercise of all four yogas. The goal of the doctrine is to liberate man from the earthly bondage of action. The prescription is to practice the doctrine with faith and without vanity.

Sri Krishna has a bold warning for anyone who might disapprove of the doctrine:

Ye tvetadabhyasūyanto
nānutiṣṭhanti me matam;
Sarvajñānavimūḍhāṁstān
viddhi naṣṭān acetasaḥ — 3. 32

SRI KRISHNA'S WARNING

'But those who, decrying this, do not follow my teaching are deluded about all knowledge and are devoid of discrimination.' He alerts people who might not understand and might not be proficient with the discipline. He realizes that all the faculties are not well developed in each of us. Faculties are built through the process of evolution. We must have the ability to recognize their existence and attempt to perfect them. We need guidance. Sri Krishna provides it.

In the beginning of the fourth chapter, Sri Krishna says:

Imaṁ vivasvate yogaṁ
proktavān aham avyayam;
Vivasvān manave prāha
manurikṣvākave'bravīt — 4. 1

HISTORY OF THE DOCTRINE

'I imparted this imperishable Yoga to Vivasvān. Vivasvān taught this to Manu. Manu transmitted this to Ikṣvāku.' Thus Sri Krishna gives a line of transmission of the doctrine from the olden days to the present time. The original recipient was Vivasvān, the Sun. Vivasvān taught the doctrine to Manu, who transmitted it to his son Ikṣvāku.

Truth is as ancient as the creation. People try to twist truth in many ways, but the essential truth never gets twisted. While no one can alter it, the 'original' can get lost because of lack of practice. Similarly this yoga, which governed all in the beginning, was lost. Sri Krishna says to Arjuna (4. 3): *sa evāyam mayā te'dya yogaḥ proktaḥ purātanaḥ*, 'That ancient yoga itself has been taught to you today by Me.' It is similar to St. Augustine's interpretation, 'What is Christianity?' 'A religion already existed. After the advent of Christ we called it Christianity. It is the same religion.' So, this is the same yoga that was there long ago. It is given to Arjuna again.

GODHEAD AND SRI KRISHNA

While establishing the eternity of the doctrine, Sri Krishna communicates his own eternal existence. We are exposed to two personalities: the teacher of Arjuna who enunciates the yoga principles, and the eternal Godhead, who has been ever existing, to whom we surrender our actions. Both the personalities are merged in Sri Krishna, who realizes his divine existence through his yoga.

Sri Krishna says in the *Gita*: 'See Me in all beings and all beings in Me.' 'We are all created in the image of God', said Moses. Christ says: 'The kingdom of God is within you.' Swami Vivekananda has put this beautifully: 'Each soul is potentially divine. The goal is to manifest this divinity from within by controlling our nature, both external and internal. Do this either by work, or worship, or psychic control, or philosophy. Follow one or more of all these, and be free. This is the whole of religion. Doctrines, dogmas, rituals, books, temples and forms are but secondary details.'

Somebody said to Swami Vivekananada: 'Swami, can't you coin a new word in place of the word "God"?' He said, 'This word has been used by many people. Let us not change the word, but give it its true definition.' By changing the word, we don't achieve anything. When we ask, 'What is God?' The answer is, 'the Ground of our dwelling'. It is not something there beyond. 'Lo here, lo there, the Kingdom of Heaven is within you' (Luke, 17:21). What is the Kingdom of Heaven? It is our very Ground, the Ground of all of us. The Pure Ground is what is called God. Our psychophysical complex is built upon that Pure Ground. What is there behind this body-mind complex? We have the Pure Conscious realm. That Ground is the same for all. The structures come and go, the Ground remains. Jesus Christ called it God, the Kingdom of Heaven. Vedanta calls it the *ātman*. Sri Krishna tells Arjuna to surrender everything to That. At the same time, he announces that he is the manifestation of the Godhead. He is the God-incarnate. Upon that Pure Ground we all are.

This deathless Yoga, this deep union,
I taught Vivasvata, the Lord of Light;
Vivasvata to Manu gave it; he
To Ikshvaku; so passed it down the line
Of all my royal Rishis. Then, with years,
The truth grew dim and perished, noble Prince!
Now once again to thee it is declared —
This ancient lore, this mystery supreme —
Seeing I find thee votary and friend.

Sri Krishna to Arjuna in
The Song Celestial by Edwin Arnold

KARMA YOGA

The discipline of illumination through work is called Karma Yoga in Sanskrit. It is the yoga of dedicated action that helps us to know more about the world and to act properly. Karma Yoga is the most important discipline from the common person's point of view because we are all actively engaged in our lives. Sri Krishna says: 'No one can keep quiet without working even for a moment. Your existence is impossible if you do not work. Therefore, O Arjuna, learn the secret of work. By knowing the secret of work, you transcend the limitations of work.'

As life directs us, we become slaves of our own actions. We are victims of our own functional level. We engage in work either out of necessity, pressure, or some external need. We have no knowledge of how to work with full freedom. It is said that there are two ways of working: one is like a master, and the other is like a slave.

When you are forced to work out of necessity or because of an impulse, you are a slave. So when do you work as a master? People think that there can be only one master and all others have to obey. No! In Karma Yoga you are the master. You chalk out a program. You create the will to work. You set the pattern and you follow it. The goal of life is freedom, and because of that, the means also have to be free. You must always be free to act. Karma Yoga tells you how to act as your own master. It is to act not like a bound soul, but like a free being. Action in that spirit liberates you at this moment in this very life. You just stand up and announce — 'I am a free soul'.

WHAT IS KARMA

Dictionaries give varied definitions for *karma*. Occasionally the word *karma* is used out of context — instead of being translated as 'action' or 'work', it is translated as 'fate'. The Webster Dictionary translates *karma* as: (1) The totality of one's acts in each state of one's existence, (2) loosely, fate. Some people erroneously confuse the concept of *karma* with fatalism. It is not so. There are four definitions of *karma*. First, any action (thought, word or deed) is *karma*. Thinking is *karma*, speaking is *karma*, and functioning is *karma*. Whatever we do at these three levels is *karma*. Second, reaction is *karma*. When we react to an outside impulse, we do *karma*. Third, the sum and substance of all our actions is *karma*. People exclaim: 'Oh, it is in my *karma*.' What is in our *karma*? It is the life's activity. We are the sum total of all our activities through our life and not just the accumulation of one day's actions. Take a billiard ball and hit it. It goes from one place to another, hits again and again, and finally drops into the pocket. The total of all the strikes lead the ball to the pocket! So it is in our life.

It is the sum of all the faculties of thinking, speaking and acting. Finally, *karma* means both cause and effect. The seed is the cause of the tree and the tree is the cause of the seed. One action is the cause of another action. That action becomes the cause of another action. Cause and effect repeat themselves. That which is a cause first becomes an effect later. The effect in turn becomes another cause and we have another effect. *Karma* contains both cause and effect.

ACTION AND DISCIPLINE

'Action' is a difficult term from the point of view of the completeness of its meaning. We observe action in nature, in machines, in animals and in human beings. The activity in nature is beyond our imagination. Nature has unlimited power and is beyond our control. We witness thunder, lightning, rain, blizzards, storms and much more. Action in machines is limited and a machine does not have its own power. As energy is fed into the machine, we get work out of it. When it comes to animals, there is the activity of existence and survival. Animals are conditioned and helpless. Nature controls them. Finally it is a big miracle when it comes to human beings. Though most may not realize it, humans have absolute freedom and unlimited choice in work. There is no limit to a man's capacity. He is only bounded by his responsibility. Man possesses the potential to do anything. Anybody can go to the market and shoot anybody. We can drop a bomb. We can destroy anything, anybody anywhere. We can also be very creative.

Because the human potential is high and unlimited, the human 'animal' must be trained properly, otherwise it can be dangerous. So we prescribe compulsory education and put children in school. A child does not want to obey anybody. He wants full freedom, and wants to do everything as he wants. We need to train him how to behave. We ourselves need education, training and discipline. It is very important in life. If you don't discipline yourself, the police will say, 'Don't you worry, come on with us'. Your 'freedom' is gone. You are conditioned by their whims. Therefore, we all have to learn to behave properly in society. Disciplined behaviour is yoga. It is the self-controlled way of action.

In Karma Yoga Sri Krishna gives importance to action. Action must be done with full control. He tells Arjuna: *yogasthaḥ kuru karmāṇi,* 'be a yogi and do the actions' (2. 48). Yoga is *cittavṛttinirodhaḥ,* 'control of all the tendencies that arise in our subconscious mind'. We need to control our tendencies fully.

LAW OF KARMA

When you understand the role of disciplined behaviour clearly, then you can understand the meaning of the human personality from the point of view of our actions. Our actions establish the law of *karma,* which appears to be exact. As you sow so you reap. It is a Biblical truth. If you do a good act, you reap a good result. If you do something wrong, you reap a bad result. You love somebody, and you will be loved. You hate somebody, and you will be hated. We are all victims of our own *karma*. We cannot deny it. More than three hundred years ago, the early settlers came to the United States. They worked hard and built the nation. The results are seen today. This is their *karma*. Anything that you do becomes yours.

Swami Vivekananda said, 'I am the maker of my own destiny, nobody else!' There is no God above or anywhere in the world beyond my existence that forces me to do anything. I am independent. I take the responsibility for my life in my own hands. To make or mar, I am responsible. *Karma* is the cause. Karma Yoga tells you how to make this life meaningful, bring simultaneous purpose, joy and peace to it. It is all in us. We are free to exercise our individual responsibility.

The law of *karma* is exact because it supports the theory of evolution. All of us are evolving souls. We cannot help it. Even if you do not want to evolve, society would force you to evolve. We have jumped from the animal to the human level. After coming to the human level we have acquired greater responsibility. We remember that at the human level there cannot be an 'I' factor. Individuality is dead. We are part of the whole. On the other hand, if we think: 'I am an individual; I do not care for anybody else', we would find that we could not exercise our freedom in that manner. There is the story of a gentleman who was walking along the beach whirling his cane. Another gentleman coming from behind said to him, 'Sir, will you please stop whirling your cane?' The first man replied, 'Look here, this is God's open beach. I am free to do whatever I like.' The second man then said, 'You are no doubt free. But your freedom stops where my nose begins!' Nobody is absolutely free. Individual freedom depends on the freedom of the rest. As I am free to exist, so also are all of you. Therefore, accept the existence of all others and say 'we' and not 'I'. In Karma Yoga the watchword is not 'me', but 'us'.

You have your own *karma*. You should not imitate, compare or compete. You have to grow in your own way. You take the help of all of humanity. You take the help of all the great teachers the world has produced. You learn from every source. But finally you are yourself. Karma Yoga tells you to be yourself.

Freedom and Responsibility

Everything in this life depends upon *karma*. Without *karma* we do not exist. At the level of thought, speech and action, the law of *karma* tells you how to conduct yourself properly. Suppose you refuse to go to school. What do people say? 'Send him to school!' Laws do not allow anyone to remain idle. You have to get a minimum of education, because society cannot tolerate a bum or a reckless individual. A single mad man can ruin a whole society. It is our responsibility to see that all are educated. Responsibility is a fundamental principle of existence, and so education becomes a necessity. Suppose there is a mentally derelict person roaming on the streets. The police will arrest him immediately. Why? He could become a nuisance on the road. He might cause accidents. He is free, but freedom without being responsible is dangerous. We teach him responsibility. Karma Yoga tells you how to be responsible. Unless we follow a responsible course ourselves, the society will force us to be responsible.

Once I went to a mental hospital to see a patient. One fellow came to me and he said, 'You are very fortunate'. 'Why?' 'Oh, they allow you to go and come back.' Then I told him, 'Do you know why? I try to behave well. I don't hurt anybody, I don't insult anybody. They observed me and they found, "Oh, this is a good fellow. We can let him go in and out." Therefore they allow me to go out and come back.' And he went inside the hall and shouted, 'Hey, I have found the secret. Don't insult anybody. Don't hurt anybody. Behave well. They will allow you to go away. See this fellow goes out and comes back. Nobody restricts him.' This is exactly true. The society does not pay respect to the person who is not controlled. The entire *Gita* is based on yoga — 'disciplined, controlled way of doing.'

Sri Krishna tells Arjuna: 'Be a yogi and work. Be a yogi and fight!' It is very difficult to put that subject in battle. Why? *Yogaḥ karmasu kauśalam,* 'Yoga is dexterity' (2. 50). It is efficiency in functioning. *Samatvaṁ yoga ucyate,* 'Yoga is an equanimous attitude' (2. 48). We have to develop an equanimous attitude and efficiency in functioning together. At the conclusion of every chapter, you find, 'this is the yoga of such and such'. Why? In yoga, disciplines are necessary from the point of view of every human being. Long before we send our children to school, we tell them how to behave at home with friends and strangers. This is good education. And those that are not brought up in this manner find themselves lost.

In life you pay for whatever you do. You all know from your experience how you came to the university. 'How could I do it?' 'I went to college, studied, gained knowledge, and now I am here doing these things. It is my making. Nothing happened by itself. I made it happen.' If you start from your home with the intention of reaching the church, you have to make it happen. It does not happen by itself. You have to turn the car on, see the signs, and reach the place. If you are not careful, you get into an accident. Getting to a destination by your own effort is evolution. In evolution, the law of *karma* is exact. Whatever you do, you get the result. If you do not do it, you do not get the result. The law of *karma* helps us to evolve and make progress to be of value. It is in our hands. We have to make it.

Some time back I went to an adult correctional institution to visit a few patients. Repeat offenders were locked up there. I asked one person, 'Do you know this is the sixth time you have come?' 'Well mister, next time I will not commit that mistake', he replied. He wants to do whatever he wishes, but thinks that he has learned. 'I will not commit that mistake, so they cannot catch me', he said.

'You have not learned anything?' I said. 'What do I have to learn? In this case you have to operate in this manner in the society.' He was fully convinced! Why? He has not been brought up well. I asked him about his parents. Such unhappiness comes when children are not brought up well by the parents and guardians. It is a big responsibility. We can have children, but we have to bring them up well. Sri Krishna puts stress on that point. Yoga helps you to develop a disciplined mind and become a well-controlled individual. If there is no control and we are not disciplined, our actions will be meaningless. A human being is the best and the worst creature in the world. He is the worst when uncontrolled, and the best when controlled. The central theme of the *Gita* is how to act, i.e. how to conduct oneself alone, with one's own, with strangers, and in the battlefield. The *Gita* is the sermon of the battlefield.

Karma is everything in life. As much as you put in, so much you get out of it. Therefore, you have to ask the question, 'What do I do under these circumstances?' You do not follow any authoritarian commandments, or be a slave to anyone. Think for yourself and learn from everyone. Karma Yoga gives you the clue. We all follow *karma* helplessly out of necessity. It binds you if you follow it from outside. How can I free myself from this *karma*? There lies the secret of Karma Yoga. Doing *karma* has to become Karma Yoga. I convert an action that I do out of necessity into Karma Yoga.

EXPAND AND WORK

Love can be two-fold. One is that which satisfies us and gives us comfort. The other is when it is confined or narrow, which makes a victim out of us and puts others in pain. If we use the same love by broadening it and expanding its horizon, then love helps us to gain more joy and comfort. So it is with *karma*. If we want something, we get some work. We make some money and satisfy ourselves. Well, that could be all right. But is that all the meaning of life? As we see more of the world we expand that *karma*. We declare: 'Not for me, but for us.'

At first I identify an action with myself, with my wife or husband, my children, and then I spread it to the community, town, county, state, the nation and finally to the international society. I do the same action but not just for myself. Yoga means expansion, growth and evolution, widening the horizon from the point of functioning. Not only for my sake do I work, but to help others! I am concerned! When you read a report about something happening in Cambodia, you get affected! You immediately say, 'Well, I shall give something to them.' Many kind-hearted people send donations. One might ask, 'You work so hard, why send it to others? You never visited them; neither will you ever see them. You do not know even where their homes are.'

Why do you do it? It is because you cannot help doing it. You are part of the whole. You feel it. Therefore, in Karma Yoga you expand and work for the good of all. You feel it and you want to do something about it. Those who feel and are concerned, they expand their mental horizon and functional levels in work. They get the products from the work, and send them to help others. Karma Yoga means that. It converts the *karma* into a discipline, a process to gain depth and realize the truth from the point of view of action.

DETACHMENT

Karma Yoga stipulates certain disciplines. From the experience of the great souls we have learned certain things that we have to do. The first and most important factor in Karma Yoga is to be 'detached'. Attachment brings misery, but detachment removes that misery. When I work with attachment, I am lost. When I work with detachment, I am all right. A slave works with attachment. A free soul works with detachment. A good example is of those who work in offices. By five o'clock you are ready to jump into your car and drive home. You are a slave to that. Suppose the boss tells you to please wait for five more minutes to finish some job. Those five minutes appear like five hours. You feel restless and miserable. Why? You are a slave. But give the thing to be done to some responsible person. He will be glad to do it. Slavery means attachment. You are attached to time and the associated objects. Keep it clear. This attached mind binds you and brings you misery. A detached mind makes you free.

Detachment is the first lesson we have to learn in life. When I was five years old my parents told me to go to school. But I did not like it. I wanted to play and move about freely. Going to school meant that I would have to sit quietly, pay attention to the teacher and repeat the lessons. At home I need not do all this. I was a free soul and could do whatever I liked. So the first objection comes when we are put to school and we do not want to leave the playground. We are attached to the easy comfortable life. But parents force us to go to school. I must detach myself from my childhood playground and go to school. Now I finish my school, I am twenty or twenty-five years old. Then I do not like to go to work. 'Why should I work?' one fellow once told me. 'Do not do it, but do not depend on anybody. Be responsible for yourself.' We want to do the minimum and get the maximum. Again, there is attachment, attachment to laziness (excuse me, myself included!). If I can avoid something, I would avoid it. Let us give it up. A *karmayogī* says, 'No! I shall not be attached to laziness.' Life becomes meaningless if you become attached to laziness. You discover after a continued period that you have gone nowhere when you are a slave to somebody. Somebody kicks you and tells you to get up. I do not want to be kicked by anybody. I do not want anybody to tell me what to do. Before anybody tells me what to do, I shall do it myself. In order to gain that feeling of responsibility I have to be detached from my own immediate comforts.

We learn detachment in our families. A mother and father raise children. They come of age. Suddenly one day the boy says, 'Mother, I am leaving the house. I am going to marry and make my own home.' It becomes a shock to the mother. 'I raised you. I spent my whole energy, money, everything. I made you a person. Now you want to kick me out and go with someone else?' But that is the way. The parents can be like slaves if they stay attached to their children and not allow them to explore the world. When you are a slave, you become miserable and you make the other person miserable. The first lesson of detachment comes here. Be detached from your children. May God bless children. Let them go wherever they want to go. Let them be happy. Bless them and let them go away.

One day a mother met me and told me about her daughter. Her daughter wanted to do something. The mother got angry and gave her a good spanking. Unfortunately I had to counsel that girl. I said, 'What happened?' The daughter narrated the incident. And then the mother said, 'Swami, I spent my whole life raising this girl. Have I not the responsibility to say something to her?' 'You have every responsibility. But she is not a slave. Responsibility means we have to be detached', I told her. 'Attachment makes her a slave. With all your love, if you don't have detachment, she will never grow. For her growth, you should keep detached and help her to move on.' Most often we forget that. The *Gita* points out: 'Be detached. Be detached from everything. Nothing is yours. Nobody belongs to you. We all have come here. We are all free and independent. We must be detached.' Detachment is the most important lesson in the *Gita*. If you are attached, your work will not be proper. It will be conditioned. That is why Gandhiji called it *Anāsakti-yoga*, the yoga of detachment.

The world teaches us detachment. A miser might get money and not share it with anybody. He is attached to it. How long can he keep it without touching a cent? He sees many people die. But he never learns a lesson. The purpose of wealth is to share with people. But he hoards it. He keeps it without using it for himself or for anybody else. The attachment brings misery.

If you examine, analyse and appraise every step in your life, you discover to your surprise that you have to stay detached. The most important factor in detachment is to include others in your life. Instead of throwing them out, include more and more. Karma Yoga tells you to widen your mental horizon, the physical field and the functional level.

Ego

Jesus Christ said, 'Love thy neighbour as thyself.' Again, he said, 'The least you have done to anybody, (that) you have done unto me.' We have to learn this. The most important part of Karma Yoga is selflessness, 'to be without ego'. We always calculate what we might get from work. How does it satisfy my individual ego? So long as you keep your ego, you will never be happy. The ego is a great burden in society and in life.

The ego is your friend and it is your enemy. A collective and conquered ego is your friend. An uncontrolled and unconquered ego is your enemy. The ego is like a dog. Let us say you purchase a dog and bring it home. What do you say if the dog does not care? Is it a friend of yours? You are charged when it runs here and there and bites somebody. You must control the dog. A controlled dog is your friend. Wherever you go and whatever you say, the dog follows you. But an uncontrolled dog is your enemy. Similar is the ego. The uncontrolled ego is your enemy. The controlled ego is your friend. Karma Yoga tells you to keep the ego under control. Do not deny it. Simply keep it under control. The ego helps you to function. At the functional level it acts by asserting, 'I can do it, I have got the strength, the power and the will.' Thus, a controlled ego is a great power. We all need it and must have it. But we need to widen it. Do not let it die as it is. We need to expand it. We say, 'not for my good, not for the good of my country, but for the good of the whole world, for the good of all humanity.' We have to expand away to the collective ego from the individual ego.

Unselfishness as the Meaning of Life

Not only must the ego be controlled and we be detached, but we have to discover the meaning of life. We pose the questions: 'Why are we all here? What is the purpose of our existence?' In searching for the meaning of life, we discover that pleasure and pain from the point of view of our own being are the same in all! This discovery opens up a new dimension in our existence. If I am starving, I suffer. So also if I see starvation anywhere, my heart cries out and I must help. If I am in distress, I feel pain. So also if someone else is in that situation, I must find out what I can do. Life is uniform. It is impersonal. Not 'me' but 'us'!

Just imagine yourself before a man who is starving. Bring a plate of food, sit before him and try to eat. How do you feel? An animal does not care. It grabs food, eats and gets out. But a human being cannot do it. You may call it weakness. I call it virtue.

Sri Krishna says in the *Gita*: 'A yogi is one who sees self-sameness in all, and equates his life with the life of all beings.' 'An equanimous attitude is called yoga.' And in that equanimous attitude, dexterity — efficiency in functioning, is the essence. Some people carry the impression that a yogi is one who is good for nothing, does not care about anything, sits alone in a cave and meditates. No! A yogi is deeply concerned, is efficient in functioning, and is thorough in every way. He is not a dull fellow. He is actively concerned. Sri Krishna tells Arjuna, 'Be established in yoga and act.' To be in yoga means to be established in harmony, unity and togetherness. Establish yourself in unity and then act.

Yoga helps you to gain this because you are going to break the bondage of action. Whenever you become unselfish, you will be more effective than when you are selfish. I will give you a good example. Some years ago, one of my friends was in a terrible financial situation. Something happened and he was about to be declared bankrupt. It was not his fault, but some unfortunate circumstances had forced him. He approached many people to help him. Nobody did. Nobody wanted to take a chance. He survived through his good offices and goodwill, and everything turned all right. Two years after this incident he was asked by the administrators of United Way to work for them in a particular field. Since he was a good and honest man, he took up the cause and went around collecting funds. One night he came to me and said, 'Swami, when I was starving and I was utterly depressed, I requested people to help me, but nobody did. Why do people help me now?' I told him, 'Do you know why? Now you are going not for yourself but for a noble cause. You are more effective now. You are more thorough. You can do more work because you are unselfish.' Unselfishness is the greatest virtue.

Karma Yoga tells you to be unselfish. If you are unselfish, your work will be excellent. Not only that, if you are unselfish and if something wrong happens, you will not be held responsible. This has been proven many times. When you fail in your own way individually, you have to bear the responsibility. But if you are unselfish and something happens, society will not blame you. They will put only one question, 'Is there any selfish motive behind it?' If not, then hands off! You are acquitted! Sri Krishna says in the *Gita*, 'Wretched are those who seek immediate results and are selfish. Great souls are unselfish. They work for the good of all.'

Be unselfish, be detached and be free from the ego. Be concerned and never be lazy. Laziness is one of the worst failures of a human being. It is a sin to be lazy. We cannot afford to be lazy. Your own growth will be thwarted if you are not active, up and doing. Laziness is something a *Karmayogī* always fights. Never yield to unmanliness or laziness, or any weakness of the kind. The human potential is immense in every individual. You have to discover that potential and manifest it in action. Karma Yoga tells you the secret: 'In all these actions you should work like a master, not as a slave.' You take your own initiative, stand on your own ground and develop the qualities of detachment, egolessness and unselfishness. Include these more and more in your life and work constantly.

This does not mean that you tire out yourself, become exhausted and die. Express yourself according to your age, strength and potential. To be active is to be living. To be inactive is to be dead. What is a dead body? It is an inactive body. Having all the senses and all the potentials, we act like dead bodies. Let us live and not merely survive.

GANDHI'S LIFE OF EQUANIMITY

Karma Yoga tells you to be a living creature, not just a surviving entity. In the living process, you must be actively involved. Mahatma Gandhi was involved in the lives of three hundred and fifty million people in India for more than fifty years. He had many problems to which he needed answers. He discovered these answers in the *Gita*. He announced: 'I call the *Gita* my mother because I get all the answers in the *Gita*. I learn how to conduct myself — alone, with my people, with the strangers, and with the enemy.' With such a philosophy, he could boldly say: 'I have no enemy.'

Once Gandhi told a reporter, 'I do not have any enemy.' The reporter commented, 'But what about the British?' 'The British are not my enemy. Imperialism is.' He said very boldly, 'imperialism is my enemy. Without that imperialistic attitude, the British are my friends. I do not hate them.' The *Gita* tells you to accept all people. *Samatvaṁ yoga ucyate*, 'yoga is equanimity'. And Sri Krishna tells elsewhere (6. 30): 'He who sees God in all beings and all beings in God, will not be separate from God nor will God be separate from him.' The *Gita's* philosophy is universal, impersonal and eternal. We have to work with this attitude. The *Gita* expresses its teachings clearly and we have to think. We have to gain depth. We have to evaluate our situation from the point of view of the whole society and act accordingly. In many passages in the *Gita*, Sri Krishna tells, 'Fight! Be a yogi first. Act in a well controlled manner.' That action, which is based on an equanimous attitude and on integrity of the well controlled individual, will not go wrong.

To be a *Karmayogī* you need not believe in any theology or philosophy. Believe in yourself and be strong and selfless. Swami Vivekananda said at the end of his book on Karma Yoga: 'If a man does unselfish work, he will know the Truth even if he does not go to a temple, or does not worship any God.' It is selfishness that covers the Truth. Unselfishness opens it. Karma Yoga has that wonderful power of unselfishness. And Mahatma Gandhi was like that. He was absolutely unselfish. He was without an ego, always concerned and detached. And he worked for the good of people. On one occasion when he was at the peak of his movement, he stopped all protest agitations since some British officers were killed. He said, 'Halt! Let us have absolute silence for a few days', and he fasted. The leaders and the masses did not appreciate halting the movement while it was in full swing. All the newspapers criticized him. Even Hitler wrote a letter to Mahatma Gandhi: 'You are no leader. How could you stop such a great movement?' To that letter, Mahatma Gandhi replied: 'I am not a leader. I am the follower of the whole country.' He was to speak in Calcutta on the day when everything stopped. He wanted to explain it to people. I happened to be present in Calcutta on that day at the Esplanade where the meeting was held. He wanted to tell people why he did not like the violence in his own camp. When he stood up, someone from a distance threw a shoe at him. Gandhi took it, kissed it, and put it on the table. 'This is the greatest gift of my countrymen', he said. That insult did not stop his talk and Gandhi was undeterred. You find one perfect example of egolessness and detachment in Gandhi's conduct.

SRI KRISHNA'S MESSAGE

The setting in the *Gita* is a battle. It is a fight between two clans who happen to be cousins. We say, 'Bad boys and good boys'. One group is bad, and another good. The bad boys said, 'We will not give anything to them. They have to fight and take it.' The good boys said, 'Well, there is no other recourse.' They gathered forces, brought armies and came to fight. They were not weaklings, but were very strong and powerful people.

Arjuna, the leader of the Pāṇḍavas, is the principal person there. In those days the battle was a challenge. The warriors were asked to come on an appointed day after sunrise and the battle was to begin. Arjuna asked his charioteer Sri Krishna to bring the chariot to the front. He was in the centre and both the armies saw him. He saw his own brothers and cousins on his side, and he saw his grandfather, his teacher and cousins on the opposite side. With his nobility he could not imagine that he had to kill his own kinsmen. He said, 'I am not going to kill anybody.' And he told Sri Krishna, 'Better to live on food by begging than get an empire after killing my people.' Sri Krishna was an illumined person and the first conscientious objector! It is he who had plainly said, 'I am not going to fight. Fighting is an evil.' But he wanted to help. He was called to act as Arjuna's charioteer. When Arjuna said, 'I am not going to fight', Sri Krishna felt the need of using some power. He said, 'Don't yield to unmanliness. Don't be a coward at this time. Stand up!' He used strong language against him. Swami Vivekananda used to quote many times the following passage:

Klaibyaṁ mā sma gamaḥ pārtha naitattvayyupapadyate;
Kṣudraṁ hṛdayadaurbalyaṁ tyakvottiṣṭha parantapa — 2 .3

'Yield not to this unmanliness, O Pārtha, for it does not become thee. Cast off this petty faintheartedness and arise!'

Arjuna was ready to stand up, but came with a big question: 'How can I kill my own grandfather, my own teacher?' He said to Sri Krishna, 'I am confused, bewildered and lost. Please tell me for certain, what I should do now. You are my teacher and my guide.' He abandoned his own way of thinking and surrendered to Sri Krishna, who stands for the Divine. When Arjuna surrendered to Sri Krishna, then Sri Krishna taught him the message of the *Gita*.

Sri Krishna tried to enlighten him from every point of view. He taught him the meaning of life, the meaning of death, the meaning of the hereafter, the meaning of individual responsibility and social concern, and the meaning of ultimate reality. He made a complete analysis of human strengths and weaknesses. And after explaining it all, he gave his best message: 'When you are in doubt, when you are confused or lost, surrender yourself to the higher spiritual values.'

Let me give a good example from American history. This is regarding the story of the Civil War. Lincoln plainly said, 'I want to maintain and preserve the union of our wonderful American state.' To that end, he asked soldiers to fight. He said, 'I do not want God to be on my side. I want to be on God's side.' They are all his own people, North and South. He initiated the fight and the Union was restored. When people were being killed in South, somebody came and told him one day, 'You know, today we committed this…' Lincoln was silent. He did not appreciate and did not take it as a big credit. He said, 'I do not want to kill people. All I want is the whole Union of the American continent restored. I want to be on God's side. God must say, 'Lincoln, you have done right.' I don't want God to approve my actions. I want to be on his side.'

Action is Essential

The central theme of the *Gita* is *karmapradhāna* — 'Action is essential'. Not what we think, or what we believe, but what we do and how we behave. Behaviour is more important than our belief, conviction and conduct. It is not our faith but our functioning. The main stress in the *Gita* is to act properly. You have to behave in this society with full integration of personality, with full control, keeping in mind the well-being of others with an equanimous attitude. Then alone your actions will be proper.

We all have to function with detachment. If we have attachment, we get greed and ego and we lose our ground. Sri Krishna repeatedly tells Arjuna: 'Be detached and work. You are not fighting for any gain in this battle. You fight injustice, not to gain anything out of it. Be detached and remain detached.' Detached action is Karma Yoga.

Questions and Answers

Q: Do I understand that the *Gita* recommends 'killing' if there is a need? This contradicts the Biblical teaching 'Don't kill'.

A: Oh yes, certainly. The word 'kill' does not imply that you have an objective to kill. To suffer an injustice is sin. To prevent injustice, you have to take an action. While you took action, someone could get killed. Killing was not your objective, but removing injustice was. You did not get into action with a selfish and greedy motive. Total welfare of others guided your conduct. Your action was a duty. Take the example of Lincoln. His purpose was not to kill. But he had to wage a war because the rebels were surging to destroy the union. For the welfare of the people, he had the duty of restoring the union.

Q: Is *karma* absolute?

A: *Karma* is a process. It is not absolute. *Karma* is not what happens to you, but how your consciousness accepts it. People say that Christ was crucified because of his *karma*. I would say, 'No'. He accepted the cross and surrendered to it. They did not crucify him. He was absolutely free. Long time back he had said: 'I am the Life and Resurrection.' Crucifixion did not hurt him at all. It is all in the consciousness, not in action.

Q: How does one create a goal when Sri Krishna advises not to think about the fruits of action?

A: Do your job well. Fulfill your responsibility well. Doing your job well is your goal, not what happens because of it. When something goes wrong, be prepared to face it. Many times, people stop doing work because they are not prepared to face the outcome. Outcome is not important and you have no control over it. Outcome results from many factors. You do not even know what factors might contribute. We only see our side of it. All actions are not rooted in one individual. We are part of the whole. We may initiate it, but contributing factors are there. If we put stress on the results and something goes wrong, we would infer that the action was useless. Not so. A job well done keeps your initiative. When it goes wrong, do it again. We must not lose courage and initiative.

But whereso any doeth all his deeds
Renouncing self for Me, full of Me, fixed
To serve only the Highest, night and day
Musing on Me — him will I swiftly lift
Forth from life's ocean of distress and death,
Whose soul clings fast to Me. Cling thou to Me!
Clasp Me with heart and mind! so shalt thou dwell
Surely with Me on high.

Sri Krishna to Arjuna in
The Song Celestial by Edwin Arnold

Bhakti Yoga

Literally the *Bhagavad Gita* means 'The song of God'. It is sung by God to the children of God so that the children may realize God. Its purpose is to enlighten and illumine us, to help us to develop towards the Divine. Edwin Arnold called it *The Song Celestial*. This song of God gives us the much-needed spiritual wealth. It is left for us to discover and use it. We continue to evolve through the process of discovering this wealth.

This song, though given directly by Sri Krishna, is not confined to a particular view, sect, class or denomination. The *Gita* gives a clear expression of the ultimate reality and God. It has the unique approach that all concepts and all denominations may fit into it. Before the composition of the *Gita*, we only had the spiritual wealth of the Upanishads. They dealt mostly with philosophical discourses. The *Gita* added the devotional aspect to the spiritual thinking.

Human beings are sensitive to feelings. Devotional practices act to sensitize them. Though we use reason to establish our opinion for discussion and argument, we use our feelings in daily interactions. The important factor in the *Gita* is the fact that one has to feel the Divine. Sri Krishna declares this feeling to be devotion and love.

LIFE AND LOVE ARE INSEPARABLE

Life and love are inseparable. Man is a loving creature. Where there is life, there is love. Take two metal pieces, put them on the table and come back after two hours. They do not move. They stay where they were. Now, keep two living creatures or insects there. After some time, you find that they come near and touch each other. Do you know why? It is precisely because life and love are inseparable. To love is rational. You show your love. Until we get hurt by some negative feeling, we continue to love others.

The best example is our children. Children are indeed creatures of love. We don't wish to restrict them and we refrain from telling them restraints. They love to do everything. They love to meet everybody, love to talk to everybody. They love to give everything to everybody. Their very nature is to love. Sometimes, what we unfortunately do is to teach them not to be childlike. When a child sees somebody and the person asks, 'Will you give that to me?' the child gives it away. Then you tell the child, 'You should not give away like that. You should give only to your brother and sister, father and mother, and not to outsiders.' Then the child begins to feel that some individuals are his own, and the rest of the people are not his own. The first shock that the child gets is: 'Mine and not mine. With *mine*, I should behave in one way, and with those who are *not mine*, in another way.' Now you have already broken the flow of love. You have already given a bit of poison to the child. These are necessary evils in life that we cannot help. For the purposes of the evolution we have to accept these. We must know the limitations.

Gradually you grow up and you begin to love people. You have many problems — ill feelings, bad results and heartaches, etc. Then you question: 'What is this love, why has God given me this love, why does it have to bring so much misery to me?' These questions form a never-ending loop. Love, not properly practiced, brings pain and misery.

GOD IS LOVE

In the Upanishads, the word 'love' is used. Scholars have misunderstood, misinterpreted and mistranslated this word. Three words are used in the Upanishads to qualify the Absolute: *ānanda, rasa,* and *madhu*. People translate these three words in different ways: *ānanda* means bliss, *rasa* means essence, and *madhu* means honey. When you visualize what the great *ṛṣi*s experienced, then you discover that all these words mean the same object. It is only love. God is love, and that is the important aspect. In the *Gita*, God is centered on love.

God cannot be approached through reasoning, but only through experience. Real experience comes through feeling. Feeling is only possible when there is love. All religions declare that God is love. Consciousness and wisdom of God exist, but the love needs to be felt. The *Gita* states that even the love that we have is not ours! It is God's love. We have His image and His spark in us. His Light helps us to gain the awareness of that love. The love that we all have is nothing but the love of God conditioned by our own mind and thoughts. Every one possesses that spark, but we do not know what to do with it. We use it many times in our own way. It is just like the heat we get from the Sun. We all enjoy that warmth. The love within us comes from the Divine and fulfills us in its totality.

DISCOVERY OF THE FULLNESS OF LOVE

When we spread this love out into the world, we gain experience. To gain the benefit of it and to make it more meaningful as a fulfillment element, we have to discover the fullness of love. To achieve it we have to move towards the Divine in its fullness. So we witness that human beings have their own experience of love. When any one of us evolves, gains depth and realizes God, the first thing that happens to that person, be it a man or a woman, is the development of all-lovingness, unconditional love. When you experience fullness, you love everybody. That is the beauty of illumination. You see the whole world as your own, non-separate from you. You accept everybody as your own because that love helps you to see the love in all. In absolute pure love, you find no difference between you, God and the rest of the mankind.

We have to understand the meaning of love — its natural flow, its obstruction, the cause of its obstruction, and how to make it flow naturally. When we begin to think, evaluate and experience, we get lost in the world. What do we do? Can we find somebody who can give us the meaning of love? Is there anybody who can illumine our hearts and enlighten our beings? Can any one show us the true path of love?

'It is said, love thy neighbour, hate thy enemy. But I say unto you: love thy enemy (as thyself). Bless them that curse you. Pray for them' (Matthew, 5:43-44). Jesus Christ, who became one with the Heavenly Father, could see his non-separateness from the rest of the people. He could identify with anyone. 'Whatever least thing you have done to anybody, you have done unto me,' he said (Matthew, 25:40). That is the love of God. He experienced it in its fullness.

So it was said with Buddha. When Buddha experienced the fullness of the Divine, he called it the Truth, the Light of Truth. Looking at the world, he loved not only human beings but all creatures! He found his own Self wherever life was pulsating. He identified with everybody. He did not use much language to express it. But he felt it. He used two words to indicate that love: *mettā* and *karuṇā*. *Mettā* means friendly, and *karuṇā* means compassion — be friendly and compassionate towards all beings.

Similar was the teaching by Mohammed. Mohammed experienced the Divine in its fullness. And when he came to the marketplace, he said, 'You are all the children of Allah. The spirit of Allah is in all of you. Don't kill each other. Don't hurt each other. Love each other.' He preached universal brotherhood. Most of us miss the inner depth of his wonderful thoughts. To experience the love of the Divine, we have to move up and realize the Divine.

EXPANDING OUR LOVE

Many times people say, 'We have seen people who have no love in their hearts.' I met one such person when she was already sixty years of age. I asked her one day: 'What is the matter with you, you are very negative. You don't see anything positive in anybody. Don't you love anybody?' 'No', she said, 'I don't love anybody, not even you, Swami, not God, not my husband, not my child. I don't love my child.' She declared very boldly to me that she never loved anybody. 'Well, there must be something wrong', I told her. 'Love is natural to us. Every life must have that love. Something has happened in your life, which has blocked the passage of that love. You should discover it. Please think about it. How did you become this dry, mechanical, hateful and anti-social person?' I did not hypnotize her. I simply asked her to think. The lady thought a bit and calmed down. She told me, 'Now I know! When I was a little girl, I was playing on the lap of my mother. Suddenly, my brother came across. My mother got up. She dropped me on the floor, walked over me and greeted my brother. I looked at them and thought. "This is my brother and my mother. She dropped me on the floor. There is no one that cares for me!" From that time onward, Swami, I hated my mother and my brother. And that hatred continues until today.' She had a heavy rock falling down in her beautiful spring of love. One negative experience blocked the passage of love.

We are all loving creatures. We all have that love to the fullest extent, but we do not know how to use it. Narrowing the love brings serious problems. It gets into competition. On the other side of that love we have hatred, bitterness and dislike. Whenever we limit the love to an object, we become a slave to that object. Instead of love helping to broaden our outlook, it enslaves us whenever we narrow the love to a person or to a thing. A miser limits it to his money. He is a slave to that money. Whenever you narrow your love to some person, you become a slave to that person. Expansion is life and it leads to freedom. Contraction is misery, bondage and death. It is not that we go out socializing with everybody, but we must keep our hearts open. You cannot say: 'I love humanity but I cannot stand people.' If you want to make your life really meaningful, peaceful and blessed, you should carry love in your heart. That is why the slogan is: 'Have love, will live.' Without love life is miserable.

We do not have to love everybody equally. You love your mother more than anybody else. You love your wife more than anybody else. But you don't exhaust your love there itself. You spread it. You love yourself. When you are hungry, you eat first. You don't have to care how many billions in the world are hungry. That much you have to fulfill. You don't deny love. Neither do you exhaust it. Loving God means to possess an attitude of love.

How do we know the manifold ways to love God? How do we know God? We can only learn from those persons who have experienced the Godhead. The world has produced many such saints and incarnations: Moses, Jesus, Buddha, Mohammed, Krishna, Ramakrishna and Zarathustra among them. These founders of great religions are all men of love, compassion and concern. They realized the truth. Their pronouncements should be understood by all.

God
The Supreme Being

Bhakti Yoga is centered on love. Sri Krishna repeatedly explains how to love God: *Manmanā bhava madbhakto madyājī māṁ namaskuru*, 'Be devoted to Me. Think of Me. Pray to Me. Bow down to Me' (18. 65). The word *mām*, which Sri Krishna uses deliberately, is not the individual personality of Sri Krishna. It is the Divine in him. Sri Krishna says:

Avajānanti māṁ mūḍhā
mānuṣīṁ tanumāśritam;
Paraṁ bhāvamajānanto
mama bhūtamaheśvaram — 9. 11

'People not knowing My supreme, divine nature, confine Me to this body, to this human element. The Supreme Being is beyond and is Absolute.'

In different ways he uses the word 'Me'. The 'Me' of Sri Krishna is the Supreme Being. In the fifteenth chapter he clears it (15. 18): 'I am that Supreme Being.' We need not go anywhere or do anything special to understand the spiritual stature of that Supreme Being. You just remove the obstruction that stands between you and God. *Yo māṁ paśyati sarvatra sarvaṁ ca mayi paśyati*, 'He who sees Me in all beings and all beings in Me' (6. 30). God is all-pervasive.

A strange incident happened in the life of Christ. One day he was helping his father with carpentry. He looked up to the father and asked, 'Father, it is said that we are all created in the image of God. Where is that image?' 'My son, you have to find it for yourself', was the reply. And that was the day when he left for the wilderness. He spent a number of years seeking and contemplating. He discovered and experienced God. He got the Light. With that illumination, he returned to society. He loved everybody. He did not do miracles for the sake of doing them, but because he loved people so much. He did whatever people wanted. Nothing was impossible for him because he was one with the Divine. When one experiences that Divine Love, one cannot but love all people.

GROUND OF OUR DWELLING

What is God? Many think God is outside in the heavens. This is not the case. I shall give you a new definition of God. G-O-D is the 'Ground of Our Dwelling'. God is in all of us. You have to learn to love all people. It does not mean that you deny your personal love. Everything is acceptable.

People used to ask Holy Mother, Sri Sarada Devi: 'How do you know such and such person realized God?' Mother used to say: 'You will find the person to be unselfish, all-loving and deeply concerned for the well-being of others.'

That is the complete identity. A mother becomes unselfish, all-loving and deeply concerned for the child. One must be like that. The love of the mother comes only when you are illumined. In this path of devotion Sri Krishna tells us how we can gain that illumination. He explains many times: 'Pray to Me.' In this 'Me', there is no limitation.

Ye yathā māṁ prapadyante tāṁstathaiva bhajāmyaham;
Mama vartmānuvartante manuṣyāḥ pārtha sarvaśaḥ — 6. 11

'By any method that you think of God, you think of Me. People follow my path in various ways.'

There is only one God. He reaches you in your own way. There is no particular way. Somebody asked Sri Ramakrishna, 'Sir, how should we pray?' 'Pray as you feel from within. He is in your heart. He will hear that voice', he said. 'Make a sincere honest prayer; he will respond.' That is exactly what Krishna said in the *Gita.* Pray as you feel, to any form, in any way. When you pray to God, He will reward you. But you must be sincere, earnest, honest and serious. All forms are good. He says, 'You worship anyone, your prayer reaches Me.' The Upanishads said: *Ekam sat viprāḥ bahudhā vadanti,* 'One truth, people call it by various names.' Sri Krishna identifies himself totally with the Ground: 'Worship Me in any way you like. All ultimately reach Me.'

WORSHIP OF FORMLESS GOD

How to reach Him? People are not just interested in personalities, in forms. How about the formless aspect? Arjuna asks a question (12. 1), 'Well, who is well versed in yoga: the man who thinks of God as Absolute and Formless, or one who thinks of God manifested in a particular individual form?' Sri Krishna clearly replies, 'The embodied individual cannot think of God as a formless one.' When you are confined to this body, you cannot think of God except through a form:

Kleśo'dhikatarasteṣāṁ avyaktāsaktacetasām;
Avyaktā hi gatirduhkhaṁ dehavadbhiravāpyate — 12. 5

'The difficulty of those whose thoughts are set in the Unmanifested is greater, for the goal of the Unmanifested is hard to reach by the embodied beings.'

Many people boast: 'I am an *advaitin*. I want the Absolute.' They are completely ignorant. They do not know what is meant by *advaitin* or *dvaitin*. When you use the word 'I', you are confined to the individuality. You may have the intellectual concept but you lack the spiritual awareness. Therefore Sri Krishna says here, it is very difficult for the embodied soul to think of the Absolute as formless. One may continue to adore the form aspect of the Divine.

Worship of God with Form

What is the form aspect of God? Those who are illumined, both men and women, stand before us as divine images. For many, this is difficult to understand. When the human being gets illumination, the humanness is replaced by the Divine. People get afraid: 'How can we call a man God?' When man is illumined, his human limitations disappear. 'I and my Father are One.' We call Christ, God; Buddha, God. When you declare no separation from God, you merge with God. Let me give a good example. Take a piece of iron. Put it into fire. Make it red-hot. Take it out and show it to people. What is that? It is fire. It is red-hot. It looks like fire, and it works like fire. We say it is fire!

Many times we have such narrow feelings about the Divine that we cannot accept others as valid spiritual individuals. All illumined souls are representatives of the Divine. It is like any red-hot metal, whether it is brass or iron or something else. We see only the fire. So also is the Divine. Born anywhere, when he or she is illumined, you find in him or her the Divine. Because there is only one Divine, it is in all of us. We do not see it because it is inside of us.

HOW TO PURIFY OURSELVES

When we look within we see only our mental clouds. We have to remove the mental clouds and purify our inner self. The Kingdom of God is within us. We are all created in the image of God. The Vedanta says: 'The *Ātman* is within us.' And Sri Krishna presents beautifully how to gain the knowledge of God and how to become one with it. 'I am in every heart', he says (10. 20); 'I am that Light, I am that Life. I am that Love in all souls' (15. 12-13). You can discover and can gain illumination now, provided you purify your heart. Jesus says: 'Blessed are the pure in heart.' Sri Krishna explains in the twelfth chapter, how to purify ourselves in order to gain depth and to realize God. The most important factor, as stated before, is love. You must love to work, but the work must be unselfish. Without love, life is useless. So also you must love the Supreme. Here the word love has a different meaning. 'Love' means, your whole being moves towards the object of love.

From the thirteenth to the twentieth verse in the twelfth chapter, Sri Krishna provides the prescription for a good devotee. In the first of these he says:

Adveṣṭā sarvabhūtānāṁ
maitraḥ karuṇa eva ca;
Nirmamo nirahaṅkāraḥ
samaduḥkhasukhaḥ kṣamī — 12. 13

'He who has no ill-will to anybody, who is friendly and compassionate, who is free from egotism and self-sense, even-minded in pain and pleasure, and patient' is a good devotee. The first word used is *adveṣṭā,* 'he who does not hate anybody'. The most important qualification of a devotee is that he does not hate anybody. To deserve God's grace, you must not hate anybody and you must be friendly and compassionate towards all. Christ enunciated: 'Love thy enemy. Bless them that curse you. Pray for them.' That is the first condition: *adveṣṭā,* 'don't hate anybody'.

Then you become *maitraḥ karuṇa eva ca,* 'friendly and compassionate'. Before you love God, before you move towards Him, you must love all people. Among the two commandments, 'Love God with all thy heart, soul and might', and 'Love thy neighbour as thyself', the second commandment actually has more force than the first. If you cannot love whom you can see, how can you love somebody you don't see? Wherever you are, be unselfish and loving. Always be concerned. You evolve gradually. Your loving capacity increases and you do not hate anybody. To love God you have to love your neighbour first. If love is not there, you can forget about God.

Sri Krishna says that in the path to Bhakti you should love all people and widen your heart. Then whatever you do, you gain the right experience. Don't consider anybody as separate; only separate yourself from the body. I enclose this same Divine Ground with my body-mind complex. I call it 'me'. In us, the life principle is God. *Jīvanaṁ sarvabhūteṣu,* 'I am that life principle in all living creatures'

(7. 9). Jesus Christ said, 'I am the life' (John, 11:25). Wherever you find life, it is the spark of the Divine. We do not feel it because we have not experienced it. Those who experience it see that we are all the same.

God is love, love is Truth, and Truth is all-pervasive. Love is experiential and communicable. So in Bhakti Yoga, when you want to spread this love beyond the individual or even a small group, we have to love the totality, the Ground. In Bhakti Yoga certain techniques have been mentioned — adoration, worship, prayer, ritual and meditation. You find these in all religions. Religious prayer is a very important practice. Prayer makes an attempt to let us feel all-pervasive. Our prayer to the Lord should be: 'Our Father..., forgive them that trespass against me as You forgive me.' In all these religious activities, what we show is the unlimited loving consciousness spread all around. The more we think of the illumined personalities, the more we imbibe their spirit. It is just like when you want to get warmth, you go near a fire and sit there. You get that warmth. If you want to gain that loving consciousness, you must worship a person of that deep all-pervading love. Then the mind, which is a tool in the entire process, imbibes that spirit of love.

Swami Vivekananda once said: 'The mother doesn't think of herself when a child is in danger on a street. She jumps to rescue him.' That is love. Love is blind. You do not care and you do not calculate. You jump there. You must love all your work. While we were working on a hospital project in India, one of the disciples of Swami Vivekananda happened to walk with us. He would alert us: 'Do you love the work? If you don't love it, don't go.' We all stood there and heard his words: 'If you do not love it, do not go.' You must love it. Then only it becomes a discipline that helps you to evolve. Love is the centre of life. Whatever you do, love it. Love is the centre in all yoga. That is why it is God-centric. Sri Krishna says: 'You must love Me with your full heart. Be devoted to Me. Worship Me. Pray to Me.'

Many times people isolate themselves. Suppose you go and tell a lady, 'I love you but I hate your children', you have to be careful and must be ready to run away. If you say, 'I don't love you but I love your children', she will be compassionate. God's children are like that. If you tell God, 'I hate your children but I love you', 'Get out!' he would say. It is natural. Sri Krishna tried to explain that as you move vertically towards the Divine, you spread out horizontally. Then the discipline becomes meaningful. Denying this you don't move up. Accepting this, you accept humanity and move up. And that is a new religion given by Sri Ramakrishna, Holy Mother and Swami Vivekananda. This is based on Sri Krishna's *Gita*, Jesus' Gospel, Moses' Torah. If you want to purify yourself, you start from here and move up. Then you get something out of it.

LOVE AND SERVICE

Swami Vivekananda removed the word 'renunciation' from the spirit of the new mission he created. 'You don't renounce anything', he said. 'Nothing belongs to you. What do you have to renounce? You add', he said. One of the direct disciples of Swami Vivekananda said to the new Swamis: 'You add the whole to your little family. You expand. You widen your mental horizon and your heart.' This was a new monastic order. In order to love and serve, the best field for a monk is education and health. Keep this concept in mind: 'Humanity is nothing but a representation of the Divine in various forms.' We do not know the Truth in us, but the illumined persons tell us: 'That thou art.' You have to find out what is That you are? The path is LOVE and SERVICE.

There is a saying: *yat sādhana, tat siddhi*, 'What you cultivate, that you become'. If you go to the slums and think of negative things and violence all the time, you imbibe that spirit and act like that. When you think of love, purity, holiness, then you imbibe them. Your whole personality moulds itself in that manner because you develop according to your thoughts. Bhakti Yoga tells you to cultivate this kind of attitude — to see God in all, to love all beings as God, who exists equally in every being. You worship God, pray to God, adore God and offer everything to God. The word 'God' is not restricted to any particular religion. It makes you evolve according to your faith, conviction and belief. You must be free.

EXPAND IN LOVE

Character and spirituality cannot be learned from the books. You have to acquire them from somebody. We must see an exemplar, and then catch it. 'Oh, here is an example. I shall follow it.' You have to find out an example in your own way, according to your own understanding and religious thought, following your own inner feeling. You have to put your heart and soul there. Make that individual's life an example to you and spread your loving consciousness. Never destroy love and never narrow your loving consciousness. That is the essence of Bhakti Yoga — to expand, to increase the content of love, to pour out your heart's love for the good of all which ultimately illumines you, broadens your mind, makes you feel all-loving. Go anywhere with this attitude, you will never be lost. You will be accepted in every society. Do not confine yourself to any religion, any creed, any sect, or to any dogma. Spread love among all. All human beings are God's children.

GREAT TEACHERS AND THEIR TEACHINGS

The great souls have come to fulfill. They do not negate and destroy. They are all great scientists. We can call the process the science of love, or the science of life and soul, or the science of the human being. They taught us but we have narrowed their teachings down. As scientists we do not fight, but as religious followers we fight out of ignorance. We have to be aware of that ignorance and avoid it. We have to spread that loving consciousness. Every soul, every living person is our neighbour. Even the ants, the lowly creatures are our neighbours. Buddha said: 'Our love must be extended to all creatures.' Why? Life is present there also. You press an ant and it is killed. Did you ever see how it suffers? What if somebody pressed your heart? Buddha said: 'What right do you have to destroy any life? Not that we can avoid it, but do not do it intentionally. Do not destroy life for your own pleasure.' He loved all creatures. When he had that illumination, he looked at the world outside. He saw in all beings the light of Truth shining. Jesus said: 'I am the life.' Mohammed declared: 'The spirit of Allah is in all.' So also Buddha saw it. Sri Ramakrishna experienced it. When he came down from God-consciousness, somebody asked him: 'Sir, what do you see when you open the eyes?' He replied: 'I see the same God in all beings. We are all children of God.' He went on bowing down to everyone.

Bhakti Yoga tells you to make these personalities the ideal of your life. We have to learn from them. We must follow their teachings and discipline our lives. We must spread our loving consciousness. If we enhance that loving consciousness through prayer, good works, worship and rituals, then we will really enjoy life.

PURITY OF MIND

The most important factor in Bhakti Yoga is purity of mind. Love is always limited when thoughts are impure. Purity of mind means purity of thought, word and action. Then alone you can experience the Godhead. Jesus Christ said: 'Blessed are the pure in heart for they shall see God.' You purify your heart and mind through devotion and love. There is no element in the world that can purify your consciousness better than love. Bring love and you are purified. Love is the most important factor that is close to every human being, to every living creature. Bhakti Yoga tells you to hold on to that love and use it to purify your mind.

The central theme in all religions is loving consciousness because it ties us together. It holds us together, makes us feel like one big human family — one world, one existence, one Godhead, one life. We are all participants in the same life. There are not many lives, but the same life is shining in every being. It is just like space. Space is one, not divisible. All the planets are there in space, within and without. So also, we exist as part of one life. We are like so many bubbles in that loving consciousness. It is possible that this bubble could burst in one or two seconds, and we would go back to God. From God we come, in God we stay, to God we go back. God is that loving consciousness.

Bhakti Yoga tells you to follow spiritual techniques according to your own individual development and frame of mind. But the most important thing is to expand your consciousness. 'Who is dear to Me?' 'He who loves all beings equally is dear to Me', says Sri Krishna. He adds: *Samatvaṁ yoga ucyate,* 'Equanimous attitude is called yoga.' Pain and pleasure are the same to a yogi. That loving consciousness makes you equal. Here is a mother having four or five children. What is her attitude towards the children? 'They are all mine.' She cares for them. She loves them. She is concerned, because it is herself multiplied. We are all children of God. A mother tells her children, 'Mary, take care of John. John, take care of Mary. You are brother and sister.' Then they behave well as brother and sister. So also, these great souls like Jesus, Buddha, Krishna, Ramakrishna and others told us: 'You are all children of God. Behave well.'

FREEDOM

And now comes the most important factor that leads to liberation and freedom. What you learn as a child, that these are mine, and those are not mine, is not true any more. You grow up. Fortunately you move about in different societies. You discover to your surprise and shock that you should rather expand. You have to begin to love all people with knowledge and experience, and not continue to be an ignorant-child. What you learned as a child, you have to unlearn now. You have to learn a new technique. You grow up to love all people.

In Bhakti Yoga, spreading this loving consciousness in many ways helps us to gain freedom. We are bound emotionally. We are free only when our emotions are spread out and not narrowed down. There are different religions and different disciplines, but the main teaching is this: Spread your loving consciousness equally. Make it all-pervasive. Then you enjoy life better. Wherever you go, you don't feel sorry. You do not feel disappointed because you love them also. The Holy Mother, Sri Sarada Devi, Sri Ramakrishna's wife, said in her last message, before she passed away: 'No one is stranger to you, my child. Make everybody your own. We are all God's children. Do not look at the faults of others. Find out your own limitations and love all people. Be concerned!'

The truth about Bhakti Yoga lies in the practice of devotion. Be devoted to one and all. It is difficult but we have to practice it regularly. Tell yourself day in and day out: 'From me let there be no danger to anyone who lives.' No one is to be blamed. Real religion means spreading your loving consciousness. It doesn't matter if one is a Muslim, a Hindu, a Buddhist, a Christian or a Jew. You respect them all and learn from all. Imbibe that loving consciousness and then be blessed. Be happy, and be free. Otherwise you cannot go beyond the Christian group, you cannot go beyond the Islamic group or the Jewish group, because you love only that group. Be a citizen of the whole world. We have to learn to love people in spite of their limitations. I love because I have love in my heart. As the sun shines on all, good and bad, the sinner and the saint, so let love come from inside of my heart and accept everyone.

I will tell you a story in Mohammed's life. He used to run away whenever there was a fight. One day, he ran away and was hiding under a bush. One of his opponents saw him and came on horseback with a sword and put it at his neck. 'Who can save you now?' he asked. Mohammed shouted, 'Allah'. He shouted in such a way that the man dropped the sword. Then Mohammed took it and put it at the neck of that man, his enemy. 'Now who can save you?' 'No one!' Then he returned the sword to the man and told him, 'Be merciful!'

LOVE ALL

'Oh Lord, Oh Lord, I don't know you' (Matthew, 7:21-23). Simply by saying 'Lord, Lord', the Lord doesn't come and appear before you. You have to love all people. Devotion to God and love of humanity are not two separate things. They are identical. If you want to be religious and spiritual, then you have to start at the human level. To love God means to love humanity. Then love of God becomes meaningful and you gain spiritual depth.

Buddha said there is life in everything we see. 'There is Truth in the minerals, Truth in the plants, Truth in the creatures, Truth in the human beings.' He did not use the word God. He called it Truth. He saw it everywhere, in all. 'Truth is hidden, but it is there.' Buddha's explanation about the Ultimate Reality is a grand one. It is not a mere intellectual concept, it is an emotional spiritual feeling. That is why he said: 'Hatred cannot be conquered by hatred but is conquered by love alone.'

RITUAL AND WORSHIP

All religions, without exception, teach aspects of Bhakti Yoga. In every religion, there is meditation, prayer, worship and ritual. Go to a church; there is so much ritual. Go to a temple; there is so much of ritual. It looks meaningless from outside. When you get into the very pattern of it and learn the psychology and the spiritual aspect, you discover to your surprise that there exists a great positive element. You discover a loving element. We need to appreciate and imbibe the spirit.

We are all creatures of ritual. Many times we condemn the rituals of others as meaningless, but we have our own ritual. This very dress is ritual. It is a superstition to me. I may have many other such superstitions. My food, my dress, my way of moving, are all part of the ritual. When I come to society, I have to follow rituals. We must not be afraid of rituals but understand the meaning behind each ritual.

Worship should also be treated in the same manner. We all worship; it is in our blood. We always adore something. A student adores his professor. A musician adores another great musician. We are all persons of adoration because we want to learn something, imbibe something. We must not be afraid of following our object of adoration. You should feel proud and bold when you engage in worship. Let no one condemn you. 'Let all others do it their way, I shall follow my own way.' Follow your own way and help others to follow their own. Broadening the mind is what is meant by worship.

There are so many ways of worshipping. Hindus take flowers, fruits and incense and put them on the shrine. They adore a personality. Some try to imbibe the spirit of Krishna, Buddha or Ramakrishna. 'May I be like you. May I follow your teachings. May I imbibe that spirit that is within you that you have taught us.' That is the prayer people chant. In this way, Christians pray to Christ, and similarly in other religions. In all our prayers, in worship and in all rituals, the central figure is the loving personality that unifies the whole world.

Bhakti Yoga is centered in the loving consciousness. We approach God with the faculty of our emotion, love and feeling. Instead of becoming a slave, we become free and spread love all around. We begin with God, and end in humanity. Or, we begin with humanity and end in God. Take it any way you like; but spread your entire life to that loving consciousness. Make your life the centre of that love from where love flows. Bhakti Yoga helps us and frees us from the narrowness of the emotions. But do not condemn those who are limited and narrow. May God bless them. They have their reward. But you should move up. Even then, you should not hate them. Still we have to love them because we are all travelling not from error to truth but from lower truth to higher truth. We must rather be generous to others. As Thomas Kempis mentions in *The Imitation of Christ*, we excuse ourselves and accuse others. He tells there: 'No, excuse others and accuse yourself.' Be generous to all with that loving consciousness. We all need it because love is our very nature. Let us not cripple it or narrow and confine it to a place or a person that could destroy our growth. All growth is due to that love.

There is a hymn in the Upanishad: 'The whole world is held by love alone.' The gravitational pull in matter is nothing but love! When you find two persons coming together and shaking hands, there is that love. In matter we call it adhesive force, in human beings we call it love. The same love is functioning in and through all. The whole universe is held together because of that love. Let us be part of that whole universe. Let us learn to love everyone. Let us cause an expansion of heart, with the inclusion of all.

LOVE IS ABSOLUTE

The Bhakti Yoga of the *Gita* is a very unique path. It includes all disciplines that are presented to us from the point of view of God, human struggle, love and devotion. The path of devotion as presented in the *Gita* is not confined to rituals alone, but functions throughout our life and in all stages of life. The path of devotion requires us to be unselfish and to be loving. It is easy to realize the Divine. The Divine is Loving Consciousness. Consciousness is all-pervasive and love, and when purified, it gains depth. That is why God is love and love is the Absolute.

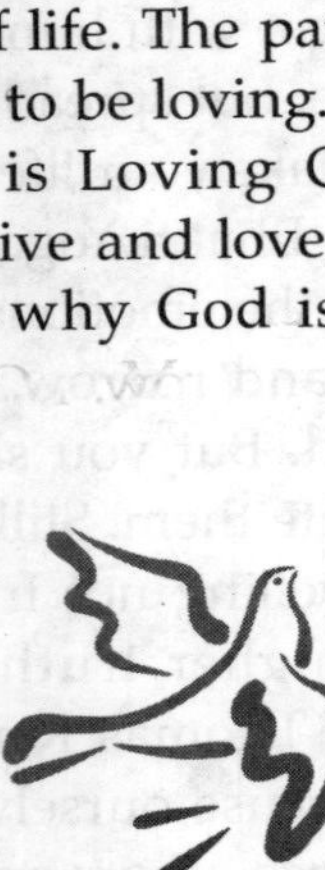

Questions and Answers

Q: It is so much easier to love people who you like and who you get along with. What about people who are really at odds and don't like you and really do bad things to you?

A: There is one thing we have to do. Whenever you see something, remember Christ, remember Krishna: 'I am the Life.' If God exists in that person, why he or she does like this? There must be something wrong and the individual does not know. He or she behaves badly because of ignorance! You should not hate. The cause is ignorance. So, in spite of the bad actions by the person, you return love. When you love, try to find out how you can help. If people hate you, you have to put two questions before yourself: Did I do anything to hurt them? Or, have they misunderstood? But in all cases, never hate them, not for their sake, but for your own sake.

Q: Is it not easier to love people through my intelligence rather than my feelings?

A: Call it the rational approach. If you are really rational, you feel. Intelligence is a misunderstood word. Anything that discriminates, separates, is not intelligence. Intelligence gets to the root of things, the cause and the effect. When you go to the root of things, you discover that is not intelligence. It is love.

Yea! Son of Kunti! for this flesh ye see
Is Kshetra, is the field where Life disports;
And that which views and knows it is the Soul,
Kshetrajna. In all 'fields,' thou Indian Prince!
I am Kshetrajna. I am what surveys!
Only that knowledge knows which knows the known
By the knower! What it is, that 'field' of life,
What qualities it hath, and whence it is,
And why it changeth, and the faculty.
That knoweth it, the mightiness of this,
and how it knoweth — hear these things from Me!

Sri Krishna to Arjuna in
The Song Celestial by Edwin Arnold

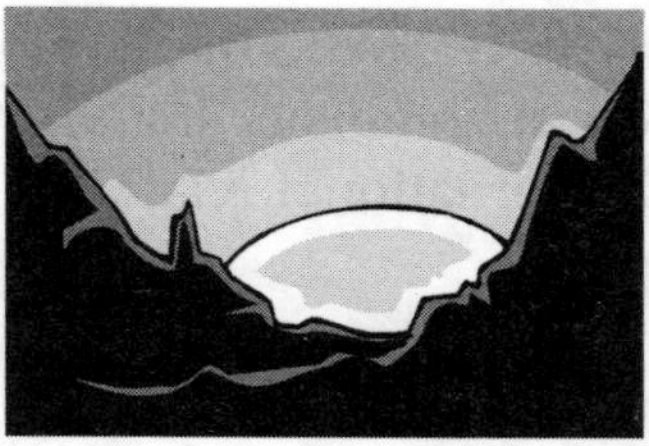

Jnana Yoga

Wisdom is the ultimate goal of life. Knowledge about events and things furnishes us with only bits of information. What we procure from that knowledge is wisdom. Knowledge is necessary, but it is wisdom that guides us in life. The approach of the *Gita* from the standpoint of wisdom is unique. We may ask: 'What is wisdom?' When you combine the knowledge of the external world with the knowledge of the internal, you get wisdom. Jnana Yoga is the yoga through wisdom.

The main purpose of yoga is to make us free from human limitations and gain awareness from within in order to perfect all our faculties. We have seen how we can perfect and widen our faculty of feeling, deepening it beyond our simple individuality and merging it in God. By developing the faculty of willing through psychic control, the great potentialities of the mind can be unfolded from within and we become aware of a wider world, which brings meaning to life here and now. The question is: 'What is the truth about our real nature?' Here we are thrown in the world situation. We have to move and relate ourselves to all people because we are a part of the whole. In order to relate properly and to understand others we have to know what we are. We remember the Delphi Oracle: 'The highest wisdom is to know thyself.' We are individuals with the rest of the mankind — with our brothers and sisters at home, our friends outside, and with our national and international relations. We are indeed a part of humanity.

WHAT IS THE TRUTH

For two thousand years, the Indo-Aryans spent their life and energy to discover self- knowledge. In all the Upanishads, the main questions have been: 'Who is this human being? What is his true nature? How does he function? What is the ground of his personality?' The questions analysed in the Upanishads are non-dogmatic, non-creedal, non-sectarian, universal and impersonal in their approach. The *Gita* draws its message from the Upanishads. The whole discipline is a search for the truth. It is said: 'Know the truth and it shall make you free.' If you know what you are, then you know the truth about every person.

In this process, the first question always is: 'Is it true?' A scientist asks, 'Is it true? Is it a fact or fiction?' If it is a fiction, he does not care. If it is a fact, he cares for it. He examines, analyses, appraises, evaluates and then possibly discovers something. Similarly, in the quest of spirituality, the first question is: 'What is the truth?' Truth is the same at all times and under all circumstances. It is the same yesterday, today and tomorrow. It is the same to you, to me and to anyone in this whole world. It does not change. In order to find the truth, Sri Shankaracharya gives us a four-fold discipline. First, to know the truth and to know the self, one should constantly question: 'Is it true?'

Second, one should put off that which is not true and not permanent. One should have the boldness, courage and will to say 'no'. The third discipline consists in following the practices of self-control. The fourth discipline is to create a desire to be free so that we are not enslaved by others.

HOW WE GAIN KNOWLEDGE

To understand the world, we have to gain knowledge. There are three disciplines to gain knowledge: *śravaṇa*, *manana*, and *nidhidhyāsana*. *Śravaṇa* means to hear. We are all born ignorant and we have to learn. So the first step is to hear, read or observe. Second is *manana*: to think about it, reflect on it. Thinking is a great art. The dictionaries define it variously as pondering, discriminating, knowing, analysing, examining, reasoning, measuring, etc. None of these however explains what thinking is. Thinking is the art of contemplating and correlating ideas, thoughts and facts. What you hear, what you read, and what you observe have to be correlated carefully. Most times it is done unconsciously. Suppose all the parts of a machine to be assembled are in front of you. What do you do there? You start thinking — how to correlate them, put them in the proper place and make the machine work. Similarly, a scientist gets all the facts, correlates and puts them together and then waits. Einstein was once asked how he could discover so many things. He replied, 'By a vision'. How did he get a vision? He got all the facts from nature, observed them and then spent a lot of time correlating them properly and then waited. *Nidhidhyāsana* is the process of contemplation, meditation and fusion. Then you get the vision.

Let us take the example of Newton. Newton saw an apple falling down. He asked why things fall down. What is wrong with them? Why don't they go up? All things fall down. Now he has to relate these observations. Here are the apples above falling down on the ground. Everything is falling down. There must be some pull from below to draw things there. He observed, thought, contemplated and then discovered the law of gravitation. He observed things just as Einstein did later. He had the wonderful power of correlating things and he discovered many laws. He could prove some mathematically, but he did not have time to prove a few others. This is *nidhidhyāsana*, the third step in gaining knowledge.

Whenever you think on a problem, you have to collect all the facts and ask yourself, 'Have I obtained everything?' When you do, you should put them all together. After you have them in your brain, the subconscious mind starts working and after some time the answer might come in a flash. Knowledge in the *Gita* is similar. It is both contemplative and visionary. It helps you appreciate the subtleties in an easy manner.

In this life of ours we have to think about what is true and permanent and what is not true. We have to examine our own personality. The Upanishads ask, 'Who are you?' Here we are with our five faculties: the physical, mental, vital, rational and the blissful. They are five sheaths and they are all changing. The whole human personality is changing from childhood onwards. Many things have changed in us and we are not the same persons that we were in our childhood. The baby-body and baby-mind are gone; the present body and mind have come into being. In all these things our bodies are changing, our vital forces are changing, our minds are changing, our rational faculties are changing, our peaceful beings have changed. At one time, we put our minds on toys and playing, but now we put them elsewhere. All are changing. At the same time, we feel we are the same, and we are not changing!

If I saw you ten years back, I can say today that we met ten years ago. Ten years ago it was not the same body, nor the same mind. So there is something constant in me when everything else is changing.

THE FIELD AND THE OBSERVER

In the thirteenth chapter, Sri Krishna begins with a wonderful statement. There are two objects in this external world: *kṣetra* and the *kṣetrajña*. *Kṣetra* means 'the field'; *kṣetrajña* means 'the knower of the field'. What is the field? The entire universe of outside nature plus our body and mind are the field, since they are observed. The observer is the knower of the field.

In science we are concerned about the world outside, the field. We are not concerned about the knower of the field. Einstein beautifully clarified this point concerning the observer and the observed. We deal with the observed. We do not know about the observer. Nature at large gives us the knowledge about the world outside. Einstein said: 'Knowledge is not complete unless we know the observer also.' Without the observer, the observed has no meaning. When we approach nature outside, we don't need the nature of the observer. We have intelligence and the rational approach. Einstein emphasized: 'Without the observer there is no observed. The observed is the field of the scientists. The observer is the field of religious people. Science without religion is blind. Religion without science is lame. Science does not need religion, religion does not need science. But man needs both.'

The *Gita* approaches this in an analytic way. Sri Krishna calls the observer *kṣetrajña,* and the field, *kṣetra*. The outside field includes our physical and mental states, since they are observable. Wisdom combines the knowledge of both: the field, and the knower of the field. *Kṣetrakṣetrajñayor jñānaṁ yat tat jñānaṁ matam mama*, 'The knowledge of the field and its knower do I regard as true knowledge' (13. 2). *Kṣetra*, the external world, is constantly changing, but the *kṣetrajña* is not changing. When you know of *kṣetrajña*, the knower of this field, you gain more depth from the standpoint of human purpose. In a fine elucidation Sri Krishna says:

Jyotiṣāmapi tajjyotiḥ
tamasaḥ paramucyate;
Jñānaṁ jñeyaṁ jñānagamyaṁ
hṛdi sarvasya viṣṭhitam — 13. 17

THE SUPREME LIGHT

'He is the Light of lights, said to be beyond darkness. Knowledge, the object of knowledge, and the goal of knowledge, He is seated in the hearts of all.' Who is that observer? It is the Light. It is the 'Light of all lights' beyond darkness. The observer dwells in every heart. He is the Light. Every individual is nothing but a spark of Light. That Light illumines our senses and allows us to see everything. We get knowledge from that Light. Sri Krishna declares, 'That Light is the Divine.'

We hear about the Light in many places. In the *Śvetāśvatara Upaniṣad* it is mentioned: *Vedāhametaṁ puruṣaṁ mahāntaṁ ādityavarnaṁ tamasaḥ parastāt*, 'I have gained the awareness of that Supreme Being, shining like Sun beyond the darkness.' He calls it Light. The very first word in the *Ṛg Veda*, the oldest of the scriptures of the world, is: *Agniṁ iḍe*, 'We adore that fire' (we adore that Light). And the Gāyatri, the prayer of the Hindus, is: *Tat saviturvāreṇyaṁ bhargo devasya dhīmahi dhiyo yo naḥ pracodayāt*, 'We adore that Light. May that Light illumine our understanding.' And Sri Krishna declares: 'He is that Light of all lights beyond darkness, residing in every heart' (13. 17). In the fifteenth chapter Sri Krishna proclaims it more clearly:

Dvāvimau puruṣau loke kṣaraścākṣara eva ca;
Kṣaraḥ sarvāṇi bhūtāni kūṭastho'kṣara ucyate — 15. 16

'There are two beings in the world. One is *kṣara*, that wanes and loses its ground. The other is *akṣara*, i.e. eternal, non-changing, and it remains permanent.' Sri Krishna continues:

Uttamaḥ puruṣastvanyaḥ paramātmetyudāhṛtaḥ;
Yo lokatrayaṁ āviśya bibhartyavyaya īśvaraḥ — 15. 17

'The cause of all this existence is the Supreme Being. He manifests in the three worlds and is imperishable.' Finally:

Yasmāt kṣaraṁ atīto'haṁ akṣarādapi cottamaḥ;
Ato'smi loke vede ca prathitaḥ puruṣottamaḥ — 15. 18

'Since I surpass the perishable and am higher even than the imperishable, I am celebrated as the Supreme Person in the world and the Vedas.' As I said, the field is changing in the visible world and does not change in the invisible world. Both of them come from the same Light. Light is Truth and it is the Ultimate Reality. That Light has two ways of manifestation. One is the light of the changing world, and the other is the unchanging, permanent Light within. To get wisdom we need to know both. Scientists lose it when they say, 'We do not care for the observer'. Religious people lose it when they say, 'We do not care for the observed'.

What is Real?

Swami Vivekananda believed that Vedanta coupled with modern science is the ideal path of the future. Vedanta deals with the ultimate reality within. Science tells about the reality outside. Both are real. One appears real in a shorter time scale, and the other is absolutely real. We read in Shankara's works: 'The world is an illusion.' Sri Ramakrishna says: 'The world is not an illusion. It is real.'* Put your finger in fire. It burns. You feel it. It is real. He would convince that both *kṣetra* and *kṣetrajña*, the observed and the observer, come from the same reality. Both are Light.

When Buddha attained illumination he said, 'My Self has become one with the Truth. The Light of Truth illumined me. I see the same Light in all.' Christ boldly declared: 'I am the Light of the world, ye are the Light of the world.' And Sri Ramakrishna enunciated, 'When you worship God with name and form, and as you approach God spiritually, name and form drop off, but Light remains. That Light is not the light that you see outside. The outside light changes. This Light inside of you, God, does not change.' When he came down after many of his spiritual illuminations, people would ask him, 'Sir, what is that?' 'I can't tell you', Sri Ramakrishna said. 'What do you see when you open your eyes?' 'I see the same thing in all of you', he would reply.

Let us take up the Big Bang theory in cosmology. One spark originated some fifteen billion years back. It started expanding and became the whole universe that we now

---

* Shankaracharya says 'this world is *mithyā*'. It means, this world is constantly changing (*anitya*), devoid of an *independent* reality. According to him, this world is non-different from Brahman. In that sense it is real, for it is Brahman, and Brahman alone is.

experience. This spark contained both matter and spirit. Someone asked the scientists: 'What was the previous condition before the spark appeared?' They replied: 'The rays of light focused and came out as the spark.' As Sri Krishna puts in the thirteenth chapter: 'I am that Light beyond all darkness.' The whole universe has come out from that Light. That Light produced both the observed and the observer. The observer doesn't change and it has the capacity to observe that the field is changing. The observer, *kṣetrajña*, is permanent, eternal, non-changing, ever-itself, the original Light. And the observed, *kṣetra*, is changing and is not permanent. The Light is contained in us.

WHO AM I?

Who am I? I am that *atman* whose nature is pure consciousness. The answer is not complete. There is another quality: LOVE. Love and life are inseparable. Where there is life, there is love. Our true nature is loving consciousness. Sri Ramakrishna said, 'Sat-cit-ānanda Brahman, Sat-cit-ānanda Ātman, Sat-cit-ānanda Bhagavān.' That is the truth, that is pure consciousness, and that is love. My real nature is *cidānanda rupaḥ śivo'ham śivo'ham,* as Sri Shankaracharya puts it in his hymn: 'I am not all these things that you imagine I am. I am pure love-consciousness. I am Siva!'

OBSTACLES TO SELF-REALIZATION

A question can be put: 'If the Light is within me, why don't I see it?' It's a relevant question. 'If my Self and my being are contained in that Light, why can I not see it?' There are three possible reasons. First, our instrument of perception could be dragged out through the senses and could be busy with the sensate world. We all go to the museums, and we see something outside. We never wanted to see what is inside. Our consciousness is drawn out by the senses. We are slaves of our own senses.

Second, the Light unfortunately could be covered by the mental clouds. All the thoughts that we have gained in this life by hearing, reading, observing, imagining and dreaming are gathered unconsciously. We have little control over them. Thoughts are the mental clouds that could cover the Light. When we close our eyes and look within, we see thoughts, thoughts, and more thoughts. When thoughts cover the Light we only see the thoughts and nothing else.

And the third reason is our ego. Our identity is one of our worst enemies. It identifies with everything, but not with the ground. Suppose somebody asks: 'Who are you?' You reply: 'I am an American. I am an Indian. I am a doctor. I am a lawyer, etc.' You give your qualifications immediately. 'What were you when you were born as a little baby?' 'I don't know', you reply.

If you want to know the ego's play, I would like you to read a small chapter in the life of Harry Truman. He did a wonderful job as the President during the years he served. When his term was over, he returned home to Missouri from the White House. While he was walking around his house the next day, somebody called him, 'Mr. President'. He said, 'Don't call me President. That is over. When I was in that White House, it was like a prison to me. I identified with all the troops round the world wherever our Americans were stationed. I identified with the submarines, warships and everything else. It was me and me. Ego went everywhere. When I got down last night and came home, nobody called me. I had no identification. What happened to that identity? I am not the President. It is the Presidency that made me identify with everything. That is gone.'

We have to realize that our 'identity' is a fictitious one. Actually the word 'ego' is not the appropriate word. It should be replaced by 'I go'. Wherever this 'I' goes, you go. The ego is our worst enemy. Somebody asked Sri Ramakrishna one day, 'Sir, when shall I be free?' 'When that "I" ceases to be', he replied. Somebody asked Buddha, 'What is Nirvana?' '*Anattā* is Nirvana', was the reply. When ego is gone, there is no identity with anything.

Thus we have three obstacles to overcome in order to know the true nature of our being. The senses drag us out, our thoughts cover the Light and the ego identifies with everything outside. If we can silence these three, we need not search anywhere else. We will get illumination right away. That illumination is the ultimate reality. We can experience it.

THE TRUTH ABOUT THE WORLD AND OURSELVES

By examining the perceptual world, Vedic scholars have placed before us three postulates. First, *jagat mithyā,* the world that you see is unreal. It is shocking to many of us. If anyone says that the world is unreal, immediately we jump to the conclusion, 'Oh, Hindus believe the world is a delusion.' No! What is the meaning of the word 'unreal'? Remember the definition of truth: that which remains the same at all times and under all circumstances. In this field of matter, does anything remain the same? No. The whole body of matter outside is constantly changing. It was well said by a great scholar that the person who is talking now is not the same one who started talking. In two minutes, you cannot understand the change. Suppose you wait fifty years, you would see the change. Time is a great factor here. If you understand the miracle of time, you can understand everything.

Consider a little dry seed. By itself it is good for nothing. But throw it in the ground and in a hundred years a huge banyan tree comes out of it. Where was the tree? It was in that small seed. Time unfolded it. Similarly, when we say that the world is unreal, do not come to the conclusion that it does not exist. It exists, but it is not real, not permanent, not unchanging. It is momentary — *kṣaṇikaṁ, kṣaṇikaṁ*, as Buddha put it. That is why Jesus Christ said: 'My Kingdom is not of this world.' Why? My kingdom is eternal and immortal, but this world is neither eternal nor immortal. Do not narrow it to the physical world. You have it. We need it, we all live in it. But do not think that that is all. Go further. Have the world but do not base your entire life on it. So the first principle is *jagat mithyā*, 'the world is unreal'.

Second, *brahma satyaṁ*, Brahman is truth. Brahman does not mean any god. The root *bṛh* means vast, infinite, expansive, all-pervasive pure consciousness. That consciousness which is in me and is in all of us is One Consciousness. It is the same. It shines in my mind and in all minds. We are all floating in that Consciousness. To understand this, consider the example of space. Let us take Cambridge. What is Cambridge? Is it the buildings of M.I.T. and Harvard, or is it the Chapel? The space and the ground are Cambridge. After three or four hundred years, these buildings might not exist but the ground of all buildings remains, and it is Cambridge. This space is common to all of us. I raise some walls and call it the Chapel or the Student Centre. But the space is still the same. It is not changed. We are all using the same space. Space is indivisible and unaffected by the structures. When you remove the structures, the space is the same.

So also bodies have been built up in consciousness. I built this body and mind. We all make our own bodies and minds. What food I ate from childhood until now goes to make up my body. Whatever I have heard, read, imagined in school, in family, in society, in nature, and whatever I imbibed in all these ways make up my mind. So it is with all of you. Consciously or unconsciously, we have built up our body and mind on pure consciousness. Now *brahma satyaṁ* means that Brahman is truth. Brahman, the all-pervasive Consciousness, is the truth, whereas the world of matter outside is not real, not true.

Third, *jīva brahmaiva nāparaḥ,* the individual is nothing but God. The individual space of this building is nothing but a part of Cambridge. From God we have come, in God we stay, and to God we go back. Buildings go back to Cambridge when they are demolished. So it goes in outer space. Take this entire planet. All things come and go, the planet remains the same. No, even planets go, but the space always remains. So it is with Brahman. *Jīva brahmaiva nāparaḥ* means that this individual is nothing but God. This is the finest postulation of Vedanta or Jnana Yoga. The divinity of the individual is proclaimed. The individual is nothing but God.

MAKE YOUR MIND NO MIND

I can close my senses and sit quiet! I can say I don't identify with anything! But it is very difficult to silence the thoughts. The golden rule in silencing thoughts is to say to yourself, 'I am not the thoughts'. Put this question: 'Were they born with me?' You get the answer: 'No. They came after my birth.' It's all right as a thought; but when that thought comes to the conscious realm, it is an obstacle. All thoughts are obstacles. Sugar in the sugar-pot is excellent. It is dirt on the carpet. You must detach yourself from all thoughts. Buddha said: 'Make this mind no mind.' You should not allow your mind to pick up any thought.

Thoughts become powerful because of two reasons: interest and attention. If you are interested in a thought, and you pay attention, it swells. If you don't have interest and do not give it attention, then you forget it. Imagine you are driving on the road. You see many things. Suddenly there is a big fire on one side. You stop the car and observe the fire. You are interested in it; you pay attention. You come back home and you tell everybody, 'I saw a big fire'. You don't remember many other things you saw. Interest and attention make the thought swell. Most of our knowledge is dirt from the point of view of Light. If you have got the boldness to say 'I am not the thoughts' and pay attention to that peaceful and joyous Light inside of you, you receive illumination right within you!

The most important factor in the *Gita* is detachment. You should be detached from the ego, from the senses, and from the thoughts. Gandhiji called it *Anāsakti-yoga*, the yoga of detachment. If you can detach yourself from everything in this world, you gain illumination. You need not bring Light to yourself since the Light itself will shine. You make it a point to get that Light, which is your true nature.

Freedom
By Knowing the Truth

We must be absolutely silent. Whenever we say in meditation: 'Let us meditate on the abiding presence of the all-loving Being, seated on the throne of our heart, radiating joy, light and peace,' we are meditating on the God in us. We meditate on that Light, without any kind of thought.

Christ very beautifully said: 'One must be like a child to enter the Kingdom of God.' What is a child? A child is one who has no ego, no thought pattern, no sense-interaction. A baby has no attachment to objects. The *Gita* helps us to know the path of action, the path of devotion, the path of psychic control, and the path of wisdom, which help us to know ourselves and the whole world. By teaching detachment it provides real wisdom, giving us joy and freedom with the realization of the truth. The Bible says: 'You shall know the Truth and the Truth shall make you free.' Truth releases you from all problems and mental agonies. It frees you.

Questions and Answers

Q: Does the attainment and the realization of the wisdom remain with the individual alone, or does that individual project it onto others?

A: You see it as self-awareness. It is seen in his actions. The most important effect of illumination is the quality of all lovingness — no complaints. One is non-separate. No one is foreign and separate. Holy Mother said, 'Make everybody your own. Nobody is a stranger. The world is yours.'

Q: How can you gain wisdom if you have to be detached from your senses, ego and thoughts?

A: You gain awareness. You discover your real Self. With senses, we are identified with various temporal attributes. Such identification brings us slavery. Let thoughts flow. Let them come and go. Let us not identify with the thoughts. Identity is the worst enemy. Someone asked the Buddha: 'Is there no God?' 'Did I say that?' 'Then there is God.' 'Did I say that?' he said. Ideas are there. He never made a statement. That doesn't mean one will be inert and meaningless. Life will go on wonderfully well, more peaceful, more blessed.

Q: As we meditate on the Light, is there a feeling that is attached to that meditation?

A: When you meditate on that Light, you think of it as your own in your own heart. That is the Light Divine, which is in us untainted by any of the thoughts. There are no opinions, no concepts. There are no images, only Light. God is that Light, actually. The Upanishads, Krishna,

Buddha, Christ, Sri Ramakrishna, all declared: God is that Light. Think of God as Light. Meditate on that Light. It could be difficult. Therefore, when we meditate on that Light, we think of that person whom we adore in that Light according to our own individual devotion. Sri Ramakrishna said: 'Think of that ideal individual in that Light.' 'As you spiritually approach it, the name and form drop off, Light remains', he said. The New Testament announced: 'Raise the stone, there I am. Cleave the wood, there I am. I am the Life and the Truth. The least you have done unto anybody you have done unto me. I am the Light of the world, Ye are the Light of the world.'

Hero Long-armed! beyond denial, hard
Man's heart is to restrain, and wavering;
Yet may it grow restrained by habit, Prince!
By wont of self-command. This Yoga, I say,
Cometh not lightly to th' ungoverned ones;
But he who will be master of himself
Shall win it, if he stoutly strive thereto.

Sri Krishna to Arjuna in
The Song Celestial by Edwin Arnold

Raja Yoga

Yoga means union. That union has three dimensions: union within, union without, and union with the Ultimate Ground. First of all, one must be well integrated. Our heart and mind must be together in composing our personality. The *Gita* helps us to gain this integration. The second is union with the world. We must realize that we are not alone in this world. Our psycho-social attributes are part of the society. We are part of the whole and must try hard not to be isolated. We observe that all separations lead to suffering. Yoga advises us to be united with all — one family, one humanity, one world, and one existence. The practice of yoga helps us to gain togetherness. The third is union with the Ultimate Ground. We may call the latter by any name: God, Reality, or Brahman. We need to be one with the Ultimate Ground. This union is Raja Yoga.

In Raja Yoga, the whole process is inward, not outward. Our success is a function of restraining our mind. The human mind has unlimited potential. In this path we gain illumination by strengthening, purifying, and expanding this mind. Sri Ramakrishna said: *mane baddho, mane mukto*, 'in our minds we are bound and in our minds we are freed'. Mind can make heaven out of hell and hell out of heaven. We have to know how to tame, strengthen, and integrate this instrument of perception and cognition. If I want to see the heavenly regions, I must perfect my telescope and keep it clean and well tuned. Similarly the mind is my instrument to see my inner 'soul'. A struggling mind is the tool. An illumined mind is the goal.

MORAL EXCELLENCE

In order to practice yoga, the *Gita* prescribes four steps. The first is moral excellence. When we are part of the whole, our behaviour should be such that we accept the whole. The conduct of moral excellence is to accept the values of the society. Anything that separates us from others is immoral. The human being must be trained from the point of view of human excellence in order to achieve union. We train our children how to behave at home, with friends, with relatives, and with strangers. Training is critical during the first five years of life of a boy or a girl before he or she goes to school.

When you study the different religions, you discover that the essence of moral excellence is the foundation in all religions. In the Old Testament, Moses gave the Ten Commandments defining moral excellence. In the New Testament we get the Beatitudes. *Yama* and *niyama* are in the Hindu tradition. Buddha spent his whole life in teaching *dharma*. This moral excellence is the first step in the yoga discipline.

We say that Raja Yoga has eight limbs or parts: *yama, niyama, āsana, prāṇāyāma, pratyāhāra, dhāraṇā, dhyāna* and samadhi. The first two — *yama* and *niyama* — deal with moral disciplines. *Yama* tells you what you should not do, and *niyama* tells what you should do. This is similar to the Old Testament where there are statements like: 'Thou shalt…' and 'Thou shalt not…' etc. Generally speaking, *yama*s are common to all religions. If it were done to me, would I approve of it? People say that you should not tell a lie. 'Why not? It helps me to get more money or get away from something.' Suppose someone tells a lie to you, would you like it? Why should I not steal? Because I wouldn't like it if someone stole from me. All moral principles can be seen and understood in this way. You yourself are the judge. Do not think that God has written these Commandments and thrown them down from the sky! Illumined and enlightened persons discovered them and many decent human beings have enriched them.

PHYSICAL FITNESS

The next step is physical fitness. We all have to be strong physically. A weak body has a weak mind. We have to have strong bodies. So we come to *āsana*, the bodily postures in yoga. *Āsana* keeps you in good condition and gives you a healthy body. A healthy body can give rise to a healthy mind. Physical fitness is a very important asset for every human being.

The body-mind complex is so closely knit that it is difficult to separate. In the earlier stages, they function together. A sick man cannot think, nor do anything. The body must therefore be kept strong. That is why you find so many *āsana*s in the yoga discipline. Every part of the body can be brought under control. Unfortunately, we don't exercise that control, and so we lose. Norbert Wiener once told me in a class, 'What you don't use, you lose!' If you don't use your limbs, you lose the ability to use them. Sit quietly in one place for ten days, you will not find it so easy to use all the limbs properly. Exercise them regularly such that they all remain flexible. Our whole system is wonderful! The more you use it, the better is your health.

There are again two parts to physical exercise: external, for the exercise of the body (*āsana*), and internal, for purifying the nervous system (*prāṇāyāma*). This latter one has nothing to do with moving the limbs. It involves controlling the breath. We remind ourselves that we breathe out of necessity and nobody ever taught us the science of breathing. *Prāṇāyāma* helps us to breathe in a rhythmic way. The heart becomes rhythmic and blood is properly circulated to all parts of the body. When this is well regulated, the nervous system comes under control. As an experiment, sit quietly when your mind is disturbed, and breathe in and out in a rhythmic way, only paying attention to that breathing. Then watch how much calmer the mind becomes. *Prāṇāyāma* brings the entire nervous system under control. You can control even your brain cells by supplying blood properly to the brain.

Prāṇāyāma means control of *prāṇa*. What you see in the external world as electromagnetism has an analogue in the internal world — *prāṇa*. Sometimes, people say that *prāṇa* is the same as breath. *Prāṇa* is not same as breath. It is the vital force. The relation of *prāṇa* to breath can be understood by considering the relation of water to the generation of power. How is power generated? You have seen huge turbines where water comes through a tube with a large diameter at the top and a small diameter at the bottom. When water passes through, the wheels of the turbine move and power is generated. Water and power are not the same, but water is necessary for power. Breath is like water, and *prāṇa* is like the power. As you keep on breathing, *prāṇa* is generated. If you stop breathing, you die. Stop the flow of water and the power is also stopped!

Prāṇāyāma consists of breathing exercises to gain control of the vital force and to keep the system functioning properly. That is why a yogi must follow the technique of *prāṇāyāma*. If you don't go for the big technicalities, the method is very simple. Every writer on yoga tells you to practice sixteen times, or forty times, or twenty times or eleven times, and so on. Forget about all this! Simply sit quietly and breathe in and out slowly and steadily. That is all to it. Follow it according to your own need and capacity. In *prāṇāyāma*, you are the judge. Do not imitate anybody. Do not try to hold the breath inside or outside. Just breathe in and out calmly and steadily. For spiritual purposes simple *prāṇāyāma* is sufficient. Practice it for five or ten minutes everyday and you will feel so refreshed. You will find that you will be able to think clearly and that you don't get nervous so easily. So, with regard to physical fitness, there are external exercises and internal *prāṇāyāma*.

MENTAL EQUILIBRIUM

The third step is mental equilibrium. We have to keep the mind well balanced, undisturbed and integrated. Mental equilibrium is important in life because human happiness depends upon the mind. If the mind is not well set, we cannot proceed. The mind is the most important organ of the human frame. When the mind is well set we can gain insight from the outside world as well as from the world inside. The practice of mental equilibrium is contained in *pratyāhāra*.

Pratyāhāra means that we hold the mind steady. We must not allow the mind to run after thoughts. Every thought that comes to the mind creates a vibration — positive or negative, happy or unhappy. Ask what bothers a suffering and miserable man, he would say that a thought is disturbing him. We all evolve according to our own thoughts and are victims of our own thoughts. But in fact, the mind is never touched by the thoughts. Thoughts come and go, but the mind is always free. Developing freedom of mind is the basis of mental equilibrium.

Buddha told us to destroy all thoughts. We cannot destroy them, but we can detach ourselves from them. You can never forget any thought. Whatever you have acquired through hearing, reading, observing, imagining, dreaming — all these thoughts are your property. You can never throw them away. You can only detach yourself from them. A thought becomes powerful for two reasons: interest and attention. If you are not interested in a thought and do not pay attention, it will not disturb you. The more attention you pay to the thought, the more depth it gains in the mind.

Suppose that some negative thought disturbs your mind. You must learn to separate the thought from the mind. Logically, you already know that you are not the thought. Therefore, be a witness and not a victim. If you are a victim you cannot do anything. Repeat 'I am not the thought' always in your mind. Raja Yoga teaches you that by observing and holding the mind you can be a witness and not a victim.

When you hold the mind for some time, undisturbed by thoughts, a tremendous power is generated. In holding the reins of horses that are ready to jump, you are blocking tremendous power. Similarly, when rushing water is dammed up, what an amount of power is generated! How should we release this power? It should be done through concentration and one-pointedness. There are so many methods to gain this concentration. Hold the mind on some sacred symbol or hold it in its own pure state. This latter method is very difficult. Only men like Buddha could do it. That is why we say Buddha is a mastermind. Buddha never believed in anything — God, spirit, soul, nothing! He held his own mind and made it pure, free from all thoughts. He made his mind a 'no-mind', and in that state Buddha had a wonderful experience. In the practice of yoga, this state has been called *dhāraṇā*.

SPIRITUAL AWARENESS

Finally we come to spiritual awareness and search for the Reality. We search for the truth about our existence and contemplate on the Spirit that is common to all of us. Spiritual awareness demands that we become aware of the existence of the Spirit within us. Jesus Christ said, 'God is Spirit. Worship Him in Truth and in Spirit' (John, 4:24). The Spirit is not bound by the body and mind. Spiritual awareness, when cultivated, is both non-physical and non-mental.

At this stage come *dhyāna* and samadhi. When the body is at rest and the nerves are calm and quiet, the mind is undisturbed. It can be set on a holy symbol or a pure thought in its own state. It gains depth and power, and reveals from within the ground of our being. We discover our own reality in the process. If you ask me, 'What are you?' I would reply, 'I am a Swami, I am an Indian', and so on. Then I ask myself, 'Is that all I am?' When I was a little boy, I was not a Swami. Suppose I take American citizenship now, I was not the same when I was a little boy. Then I did not have the knowledge and experience that I have now. What is common between that baby with whom I identify and this man here? It is pure consciousness, an awareness that is constant throughout. From birth to the grave, while everything else is changing, only one thing does not change. That is why you always say: 'I am the same.'

We also feel that we don't grow. Suppose you don't look in the mirror. Think to yourself: well, what is the difference between twenty years ago and now? I cannot do certain things. That is all. Inside of you, you all feel that you are not growing! You say: 'My body has changed. I know more things now. But I am the same.' Hold on to that honest feeling: 'I don't change. The body and mind change, but I remain the same.' What is that 'I'? It is pure consciousness. On that pure consciousness, I identified myself with that baby-body and baby-mind when I was a baby. When I grew up I had a boy-body and a boy-mind. Now I have the present body and mind. I become aware of all these changes. What is the truth of my being? It is that awareness, that consciousness. You can actually realize it in meditation and you become one with it. This is called samadhi. Now I am one with this body and mind. In samadhi we become one with the pure consciousness. What happens when you realize that? Logically you see that the same consciousness is in all of us. You realize that we all are not different. What is unchanging in you and what is unchanging in me is the same. That pure consciousness is what we call the *ātman* — the Light of Truth. This is something you can actually experience. And when you come out of that state, you feel that everyone is your own brother and sister. You love them and care for them.

Behind this mind there is the pure consciousness that Jesus called the Kingdom of Heaven. Buddha called it the Light of Truth. Vedanta calls it Brahman. Thoughts cover it and so we are unable to see it. Remove the thoughts and that Light shines in all its glory. Thoughts are just like clouds; good thoughts are white clouds and bad thoughts are dark clouds. They cloud up your mind and do not allow you to see the Light behind. When you remove the thoughts and make the mind clear, the Light shines in all its glory. When Buddha said, 'I am illumined', that Light of Truth illumined him. The same Light illumined Christ. He called it the Heavenly Father. And when people said that the Heavenly Father was in heaven, he said, 'Lo here, lo there, the Kingdom of Heaven is within you!' and 'Blessed are the pure in heart for they shall see God.' Purity of mind and purity of heart are exactly the same thing. When you make this mind pure, the heavenly Light that is within you shines in all its glory. Your worldly thoughts only cover it now. That is why Christ said: 'My kingdom is not of this world.'

YOGA AND MEDITATION

Sri Krishna uses the word yoga in different ways. First he says, *yogasthaḥ kuru karmāṇi*, 'Do your work in yoga' (2. 48). We have to keep in mind the triple union, and cultivate the four steps. We have to be a yogi in our fights also. We do not fight to kill people or destroy anyone. We fight injustice. Yoga helps us to be strong and active. It does not advise pacifism or isolation. A yogi is active. A yogi remains concerned in the world and remains a part of it. At the same time Sri Krishna concludes in that stanza: *samatvaṁ yoga ucyate*, 'Yoga is equanimity'. We understand that the same Spirit is in all of us. We are the same to all. We love our neighbours as ourselves.

Yoga as meditation is presented in the sixth chapter in the *Gita*. Sri Krishna prescribes details on when we should meditate, how to sit, how to keep our posture, what our mental condition will be, how the physical condition and concentration will be, and similar topics. Meditation is a means of realization. Awareness and learning are possible only when we meditate.

Meditation helps us to gain depth. It helps us to know things and to evaluate the situation. Einstein said once, 'We scientists too have to meditate!' When we study and collect the facts, arrange them consciously and coherently, we have to meditate on the data. It is through contemplation and meditation that we gain understanding and achieve depth.

An individual has two responsibilities. First we go with the secular sense. Everything is not given to us and we cannot draw hasty conclusions. We have to contemplate and meditate to make decisions in our external life. In the internal life we meditate to know our own reality. We would discover, as Moses discovered: 'I am that I am.' When we can discover that identity, we are blessed. This depends on how we meditate. Unless we meditate we don't know.

MIND AND ITS CONTROL

Meditation is the mind focused on the reality. Reality does not consist of deities but your own Being. It is to focus essentially on who you are and what you are. We differentiate between what is changing and what remains constant. We reflect on our true nature. Krishna advises Arjuna: 'You have to control the mind if you want to meditate.' The mind has to be still in meditation. Arjuna responds:

Cañcalaṁ hi manaḥ kṛṣṇa
pramāthi balavad dṛḍhaṁ;
Tasyāhaṁ nigrahaḥ manye
vāyoriva suduṣkaram — 6. 34

'The mind is unsteady, turbulent, strong and obstinate. It is as difficult to control as catching the air.' Sri Krishna supported him saying (6. 35): *Asaṁsayaṁ mahābaho,* 'You are right Arjuna.' *Abhyāsena tu kaunteya, vairāgyeṇa ca gṛhyate,*

'It is brought under control through practice and dispassion.' *Abhyāsa* is practice and *vairāgya* is dispassion. Patanjali uses them beautifully (*Yoga Sutras*: I. 12): *Abhyāsavairāgyabhyāṁ tannirodhaḥ*, 'Arrest the mind with practice and dispassion.'

If you want to be a musician, you come away from all the rest of the activities and sit down, take the instrument and play. Coming away from everything is called dispassion. Then you practice whatever you want. We need this in every field of functioning. You will be useless if you cannot control yourself and develop dispassion.

NOTHING IS LOST IN YOGA

Arjuna asks, 'O Master, suppose a man struggles hard, but cannot realize the Reality in this life. Is he lost? Is everything gone?' Sri Krishna replies: 'No, when you struggle hard, but pass away without realizing the Reality, you will start again in the next life.' You start from where you left and you move up. You don't lose what you have gained. 'After perfecting through many lives, you reach the highest goal.'

Question and Answer

Q: Why are there so many meditation techniques? Which one should we follow?

A: Every individual is different. In a practical life point of view, every individual must be taken. A teacher does not give general instructions. You discover two things when you meet people: their limitations and potentials. We should never distort the faith of anybody. That is one of the greatest things in Sri Ramakrishna's life. Don't disturb the individual's faith. Help them to grow in their own way.

Postscript

Two profound concepts are included in the composition of the *Gita*. The first is *Brahmavidyā*, the knowledge of spiritual wisdom. The other is *Yogaśāstra*, the spiritual dynamics. In the narrative Sri Krishna is referred to as *Yogeśvara*, the master of yoga. Sri Krishna tells Arjuna: 'Be a yogi.' Such an advice might appear inconsistent since he was also counseling Arjuna to fight. He argues that if Arjuna were well established in yoga, he would not increase evil. When something is potentially wrong, it is not right to be silent. We have to protest. We must be brave enough to face difficult situations. Sri Krishna generalizes in the *Gita*: *Yogasthaḥ kuru karmāṇi*, 'Do every action being well set in yoga.' That would make all actions perfect.

Sri Krishna defines yoga as (2. 48): *Samatvaṁ yoga ucyate*, 'The equanimous attitude is yoga', and (2. 50) *yogaḥ karmasu kauśalam*, 'Yoga is efficiency in functioning.' You are successful in whatever you do when you are well established in your equanimous attitude. Yoga discipline helps you to develop a total personality. It helps you to grow physically, mentally, morally, intellectually and spiritually.

LATER LITERATURE BASED ON THE GITA

Sri Krishna has explained the disciplines of yoga in different chapters of the *Gita*. Later on, great scholars and saints in India have analysed the individual tracks and have systematized the principles. Shankaracharya analysed Jnana Yoga and wrote the book *Vivekacūḍāmaṇi*, 'The Crest Jewel of Discrimination'. This book beautifully presents what is meant by wisdom and the play of the rational intellect. The book empowers the intelligent reasoning of a human being and provides a basis to gain true knowledge. He deduces that the world is an illusion and that the only realization consists in discovering the true knowledge of the Self.

On the devotional side, Bhakti Yoga is another splendid gift to mankind. For a joyful life we need love, devotion and proper nurturing of our emotional aspects. We feel distress when our emotions are not attended to. Our primary nature is to be emotional, and our secondary nature is to be rational. We all live by our feelings. There is the gift of love to every living person and this must be properly used. The *Gita* tells us the ways in which we can use this wonderful love. Sri Krishna says to Arjuna (6. 32): *Ātmaupamyena sarvatra samaṁ paśyati yo'rjuna*, 'When that loving consciousness is there, one sees everything just like oneself' — thy neighbour as thyself (Leviticus, 19:18). This is systematized by Narada in the *Bhakti Sutras*. Popularly known as *Narada Bhakti Sutras*, it propounds methods to heighten this love, to make it pure, to strengthen and widen it, and finally gives the devotional path enabling us to accept and embrace all people.

Raja Yoga deals with how to bring the psyche under control. The goal is to purify our psyche and learn to avoid being its victim. Patanjali took this and developed the beautiful *Yoga Sutra*. The aphorisms declare a step-by-step method of assisting us in this path to the highest realm of the pure divine. The spiritual exercises needed to control our conduct are the ones that direct us to the path of meditation. Each step prepares us for the next step and each step needs our discipline and constant attention. Good conduct helps us build good health and prepares us for the path of meditation. The guided exercises in meditation lead us to the path of freedom and liberation.

The fourth path of Karma Yoga was developed into a science by Swami Vivekananda. He was bold to pronounce it as the science of *karma* or action. It is *karma* that binds us in our life and we can utilize the same *karma* to evolve and gain perception of the Ultimate Ground. We do not have recourse to the results of our *karma*, but we have our abilities in the dutiful execution of all *karma* that comes our way. Our *karma* is not a choice but it is our responsibility. To execute actions devoid of attachments is our yoga. Sri Krishna declares (3. 20): *Karmaṇaiva hi saṁsiddhim*, 'by *karma* alone, one can reach the Ultimate Ground.'

YOGA IN THE BATTLE OF LIFE

Sri Krishna said: 'With a well controlled, balanced and peaceful mind, O Arjuna, you fight.' Now, what does fighting mean? It is not to kill people, or to destroy them. It is to subdue them, to conquer and defeat them. With that aim, Arjuna entered into the battlefield. We all have to enter into this battlefield of the world with that. If you keep those four principles in mind, you will never commit any blunder. You will never lose your peace of mind. This is Sri Krishna Yoga, a combination of all the paths.

With all the different disciplines, the key word is YOGA. Yoga means integrated within, harmonized without, and unified with the Ultimate Divine Ground. Whatever we may call it, discovering one's own Self is the goal of life. Whatever religion we study, we have to study it with this ideal in our minds. By transcending religions, Sri Krishna's doctrine is a guide to all.